Pictures Past and Present

A rare collection of over 200 pictures showing the history of
Leighton Buzzard, Linslade and surrounding area.

Written and Researched

by

Richard Hart

For
Jackie
Robert and Kathryn

Text copyright © November 1986 Richard Hart
First Published November 1986
Reprinted November 1991

ISBN 0 9517663 0 9

Printed by J. H. Haynes & Co Ltd

Published by Goodwins Booksellers
28e High Street
Leighton Buzzard
Tel: 370092

Pictures Past
and Present

Aerial view of Leighton Buzzard prior to 1950, taken by Anderson's Aerial Photo Service. All Saints Church can be seen in the foreground but the Hockliffe Street roundabout, the ring road, multi-storey car park and shopping precinct have yet to be built. Notice traffic is allowed through the High Street.

Contents

Acknowledgements

My grateful thanks go to everyone who has helped by providing photographs, postcards and authenticated details of the pictures. In particular I would like to thank my wife Jackie, my sister Chris and my parents for their continued support during the two years it has taken to compile this book.

I am indebted to the following for their help: Mrs H. Batchelar, Buckinghamshire County Museum, Steven Bunker museum assistant at Luton Museum and Art Gallery, Keith Burchell of Anderson Photography, Mr and Mrs L. Cooper, Ernest Hillsdon, Alan and Jenny Hobbs, R. A. Jamieson museum assistant at The Waterways Museum, Tom Lawson, C. J. Pickford archivist at Bedford Record Office, William Shelford archivist for Leighton Buzzard Narrow Gauge Railway Society and Viv and Jean Willis.

In writing this book I have drawn a great deal from the written work of other authors and publications:

Bedfordshire Magazine;

Beds and Bucks Observer;

Anon, *Leighton Buzzard Past and Present*, H. Jackson, 1905;

Mike Aufenast, *Inn Beds*, Mike Aufenast Graphic Enterprises, 1980;

Michael Blakey, *The Story of Bedfordshire Railways*, Bedfordshire Education Service, 1983;

Alan Cox, *Odd and Unusual Bedfordshire*, Bedfordshire County Council, 1982;

Vivienne Evans, *History All Around*, The Book Castle, 1984;

Joyce Godber, *History of Bedfordshire*, Bedfordshire County Council, 1969;

G. C. Peck, *Bedfordshire Cinemas*, Bedfordshire County Council, 1981;

Robert Richmond, *Leighton Buzzard and its Hamlets*, H. Jackson, 1928;

Official Guide to Leighton Buzzard, J. Burrow and Co Ltd, 1910;

Old Leighton Buzzard and Linslade, Leighton Buzzard and District Preservation Society, 1976;

South Bedfordshire Official Guide, Home Publishing Co Ltd, 1983;

Ruth Walker, *The Story of Leighton Buzzard*, Bedfordshire Education Service, 1984;

R. V. Willis, *The Coming of a Town*, R. V. Willis, 1984.

Leighton-Linslade

Leighton-Linslade with a population of over 30,000 is situated in the south-west corner of Bedfordshire covering nearly 6½ square miles. The town consists of the larger town of Leighton Buzzard on the east of the river Ouzel and the smaller town of Linslade which lies on the west with Old Linslade located on a bend of the river further north.

London is 39 miles away and trains stop at the station (situated in Linslade) approximately every half hour as they travel the electrified line from London (Euston) to Milton Keynes, Rugby and Birmingham (New Street). The A5 Watling Street is 3½ miles away and the M1 some 6 miles, Aylesbury lies 11 miles south-west and Bedford 20 miles north-east. The new city of Milton Keynes is only 9 miles away.

Leighton-Linslade is linked with Coulommiers, France. A deed of friendship was signed in 1958 and renewed in 1982. This has enabled many school children as well as local groups and societies, such as the Rotary Club and Heath Band, to exchange visits with our French 'twin'.

The first historical evidence about the town was in 906 when it was recorded that the Danes made a peace treaty at Yttingaford, on the Ouzel. This is better known today as Tiddenfoot. Today Tiddenfoot contains a modern leisure complex and parkland, built around a lake formed from a flooded sandpit.

In 1086 Leighton Buzzard is recorded as Lestone. It is believed to have derived from the Saxon word 'leahton' meaning woodland. Over the years there have been 60 different spellings of the name Leighton. Until the printing press was invented and even for a time after, spelling largely depended on the fancy of the writer. The name Buzzard, of which there have been 40 different spellings, was added later and is derived from Busard. The name Busard is believed to have been taken from Theobald de Busar who as Canon of Lincoln was in charge of this area. The suffix is thought to have been added by clerics at Lincoln Cathedral to show that Leighton was different from the prebend of Leighton Bromswold, Huntingdonshire. In the middle of the 17th century the suffix was altered to Beudesert.

In the Domesday Book, Leighton was described as a 'demesne manor of the king now assessed at forty-seven hides (a hide is about 120 acres)'. The book also stated that during the reign of Edward the Confessor there had been only 30 hides. The Domesday Survey also records that Leighton had two water mills. After the Norman Conquest there were over 100 adult males and the market (one of three in the county) was a valuable one. King Edward the Confessor retained the town for his 'personal use and profit'.

In 1164 Henry II granted the manor of Leighton to the nuns of Fontevrault in France in lieu of money granted to them by his grandfather, Henry I. Soon afterwards a priory, St John La Grava, was established at Grovebury. The Plantagenets are known to have visited the priory and records show that Edward I signed many documents there.

The Civil War of 1644 had its effect on Leighton as Cromwell's troops were billeted in the town in 1645. In March of the same year a fire broke out. The south side of the High Street was affected. The damage caused by the fire to the buildings and properties amounted to £14,368 17s 0d, a vast amount in those days.

In 1800 the Grand Junction Canal was opened and this brought increased prosperity to the town. The coming of the railway was less well received in Leighton. The original plan was for the railway to cross the end of the High Street, near Bridge Street. However, the most influential members of the town persuaded the railway company to build their station a mile outside the town, in Linslade.

Today Leighton has managed to keep its market town character despite the changes that have occurred. The High Street has been closed to through traffic allowing shoppers to cross the street with ease. A shopping precinct, the Bossard Centre, has been built behind the High Street. This is linked by walkways to the main street and a multi-storey car park. Recently developed arcades like Peacock Market, with its small Dickensian-styled shops, have brought a taste of the 'lanes' of Brighton to the town.

Linslade is separated from Leighton Buzzard by the river Ouzel. The original settlement was at Old Linslade, on a bend of the river, just over one mile north of its present position.

In 966, the settlement was known as Hlincgelad a Saxon name meaning 'sandy bank by the stream'. Subsequently, the town has been referred to as Lincelade, Linchelade and Lyneslade to name just a few of the different spellings.

Besides being a medieval market town it was a place for pilgrimage, as a 'holy well' was located near St Mary's Church. Many pilgrims visited the holy well for its spiritual and healing powers. In 1299, however, the Bishop of Lincoln, Oliver Sutton, disapproved and issued a warning that anyone visiting the well would be excommunicated and summoned the vicar to appear before the Bishop's court. There is no trace of the well today. It is thought to have been destroyed when the canal was built.

St Mary's Church was given to the town by Simon, Baron of Bedford. In 1246 the lord of the manor gave the church and adjoining lands to the Chicksands Priory. In 1251, Henry III granted to William de Beauchamp a charter for a weekly fair to be held on Thursdays and for an annual fair of eight days 'at the Feast of the Blessed Virgin Mary'.

During the reign of Henry VIII Linslade declined. The dissolution of the monasteries in 1539 meant the spoliation of Chicksand Priory, this caused the church at Linslade to decline rapidly and with it the town.

The town recovered in 1800 when the Grand Junction canal was built and continued to prosper after the railway came. New markets were opened up. Trade increased which meant prosperity for the residents.

In order to take advantage of the new markets people moved to the area known as Chelsea situated adjacent to Leighton on the west side of the Ouzel. This soon became known as Linslade while the original town was known as Old Linslade. The new settlement soon expanded across the railway up to the hamlet of Southcott (known until the last century as Surcott or Southcote).

The population in 1800 was only 203. By 1870 the population had grown to 1,680 and by the end of the century had reached 2,157. By this time the town had its own police station and court, urban district council, as well as a church and school.

The town continued to expand but being so close to Leighton Buzzard, which was in Bedfordshire while Linslade was in Buckinghamshire, the administration and commercial difficulties became so acute that plans were made to join the two towns to form one town of 17,000 population. On the 1 April 1965 Linslade was 'moved' from Buckinghamshire into Bedfordshire and united with Leighton to form the Leighton-Linslade Urban District Council. This is now part of South Bedfordshire.

Linslade continues to grow due mainly to the demand for houses by the commuters who travel daily to London. In recent years houses have been built at Bideford Green and South-cott to satisfy the demand. Linslade nevertheless still manages to keep its own identity and is eager to keep its character and heritage intact.

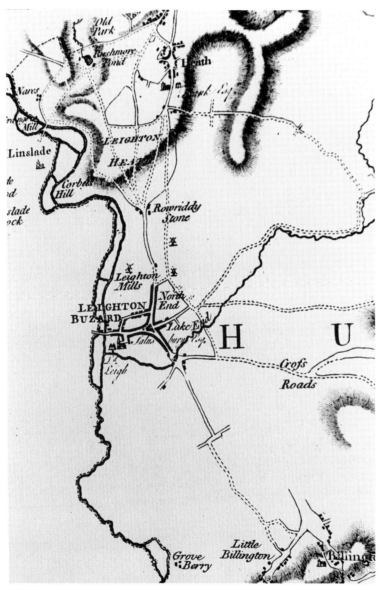

1.   *Thomas Jeffrey's 1765 map of Bedfordshire showing Leighton Buzzard and Linslade as two separate towns. Note the position of Linslade, just over one mile north of its present position.*

2.   The civic arms of Leighton-Linslade. When the two towns amalgamated in 1965 a coat of arms was subsequently adopted representing the history of both towns. The water-ouzel or dipper joins the two towns together. Two brick crowns symbolize the modern industries connected with cement, brick and sand. The cog wheels represent the more modern industries and the helmet a corporate body. The parishes of St Mary and All Saints are represented by the crowns and lilies. The bridge symbolizes the bridge over the river Ouzel and the ear of wheat on the keystone shows Leighton's importance as a market town. The motto 'By Truth and Diligence' used to belong to the Lucy family who were once lords of Linslade manor.

3.   Leighton and part of the Chiltern Hills with the Grand Junction Canal in the fore-ground and All Saints Church in the background. The view was drawn by J. Hassell and published on 1 August 1819.

4. *Another view by J. Hassell showing the old timbered Market Toll House (right) which was replaced by the present brick Town Hall in 1851. The Market Cross (left) is believed to have been built during the 15th century.*

5. *A very muddy Market Square, about 1919, showing a side view of the old Town Hall and fire station. The fire station's ladder cart is propped against the wall (right). This consisted of a hand cart with two large wooden wheels and carrying ladders.*

6–7. *Market Square before 1898 (above) and about 1910 (below). The main differ-*
ence between the pictures, other than the iron railings around the Market Cross, is the
Cross Keys (left). In the early picture part of the inn is being used by Henry John King,
a tobacconist, hairdresser and goods agent to the L and NW railway. A sign above the
shop says 'Every description hairwork made to order'. The later view shows the new
Cross Keys built in 1899 after the fire of 1898, which completely destroyed the old build-
ing. The fine building (right) is the bank of Barclays and Co Ltd, formerly Messrs
Bassett, Son and Harris.

8. View of Market Square about 1930. A horse and cart, car and lorry are standing near the Market Cross. Behind the fire station (right) are the premises of Barnabas Russell, grocer (26–28 Market Square) and Chamberlains boot and shoe makers (No 24).

9. Market Square, 1920s. Edward Pyman's watchmakers shop (No 22) can be seen (left) while the Bell Inn (now the Market Tavern) and Gibbs and Co premises are also visible.

10.   Victorian view of the High Street, 1853 with the Swan Hotel *(left)*. When the railway came in 1838 this coaching inn ran a horse-drawn bus service to the station for its customers. In 1900 the fare was 6d per head. The High Street is full of activity. People are looking in the drapers and tailors shop of Sharman and Son *(right)*. A shepherd is driving some sheep towards the Market Cross while two horsemen are making their way in the opposite direction.

11.   *Edwardian view with a more leisurely scene showing a few people standing on the pavement posing for the local photographer, P. J. Baker.*

12. Turn of the century view looking from the bottom of the High Street towards the
Market Cross. The posts along both sides of the street were used for tying up cattle and
other animals in order to keep them off the pavement.

13. This view taken about 1916 is looking in the opposite direction with the house
known as 'The Cedars' in the background. A boy is sitting on the steps of the Market
Cross watching the horse-drawn milk float. Flags can be seen displayed from the shops on
the left while bunting is in evidence further down the street. The shops of Freeman,
Hardy and Willis and Boots Cash Chemists, which are still familiar names today, can be
seen (right). These shops which were originally private houses were built from the late
17th century onwards.

14.   The back of this postcard of the High Street is blank apart from the pencilled date, 6 July 1936. Two horses and carts are present with several motor cars and vans. Gas lighting is in evidence.

15.   This picture is taken some 20 years later. There are now more cars about and they have completely replaced the horses. Electric street lamps introduced in 1947 have replaced the gas lights.

16.   St George's Day parade of Boy Scouts, 1910, being watched by townspeople in their bonnets, boaters, trilbies and cloth caps. The business of Alan Taylor, watch and clock maker, 6 High Street, is in the middle of the three shops.

17.   The Cedars (left), about 1916, with David Cook and Sons, builders, J. J. Martin's shop and the Albion Hotel in the background. This hotel, 3 High Street, was a temperance hostelry which provided a haven for those who wished to avoid alcohol or its followers. It ceased to be a hotel in the early 1950s and has now been turned into offices.

18. Church Square in 1853 with the vicarage (centre).

19. This view was taken at a different angle. The passage of 50 years has seen the disappearance of the old vicarage and the buildings on the right. The latter were replaced in about 1860 by a fine block of terraced houses. These houses were built for J. D. Bassett who offered a free annual season ticket to Euston station to encourage buyers.

20.   A fine view of Bridge Street taken about 1918 by local photographer P. J. Baker.
The Ewe and Lamb *commercial hotel is next to the printer F. W. Bendy. Drs Square and
Leslie, physicians and surgeons are at No 13 (left). The ghost-like figures walking along
the pavement are there because it was necessary to expose the glass plate for several
seconds in order to obtain a good picture. Thus any movement during the exposure
resulted in a blur.*

21.   *This view looking away from the High Street is taken by the same photographer.
The shops of John Lucking, antique dealer and Marguerite Dumpleton can be seen (left)
while the Church Bookshop is further down the street.*

22.   Early 1900s view of Lake Street with the Unicorn Hotel *(left) and the* Corn Exchange. A pantechnicon-van is outside the housefurnishers, Aveline and Phillips.

23.   A similar view, 1985, showing the changes that have occurred. The Unicorn *has now been turned into a nightclub, the premises of J. T. Webb (right) are empty and the Corn Exchange has disappeared. The vacant plots either side of Linney's shop have still to be developed.*

24.   Grove Road, about 1910. A house to let sign is in the garden of No 8. Most of these houses were built for local businessmen in the late 1870s, the date 1879 appears on No 10. An interesting feature of the street is the yellow brick pavement, the only example left in the town.

25.   Hockliffe Street with the Baptist Chapel next to the garage of Arthur Stratford, about 1930.

26.   North Street, about 1925. Above the archway is the sign of the Red Lion, one of Leighton's oldest inns. Next door to the right are Nos 3–5 with a sign above the shop front 'Corn and Coal Merchants', T. Branton & Co, Millers and Flour Factors'. A cart stands outside advertising Kia Ora lemon and orange squash. Next is the shop of W. G. Roberts, tailors. At the corner of West Street can be seen the magnificent Holly Lodge.

27.   This view is looking away from the town centre and was taken from near Holly Lodge some 10 years earlier. 'L. Croxford the smart tailor and outfitter' advertisement can be seen on the side wall of No 44 (this business is now in Middle Row, Market Square). Next door at No 42 is the shop of William Parsons, confectioner and fruiterer. He was nicknamed 'Sucker' Parsons because of the hard-boiled sweets he sold in the market. Almost all the buildings in the foreground have been demolished. Today the do-it-yourself store Fads occupies a large part of the site.

28.   Plantation Road, 1910, looking towards Leighton with Oxendon Lodge and the turning to Taylors Ride on the right. It would be rather more dangerous today for the two gentlemen to stand in the middle of the road. A wide variety of trees were planted in this area, by Arthur Ashfield in the 1800s and later by the Bassett family, which have given pleasure to generations of townspeople.

29.   This modern view shows the changes that have occurred. The muddy road has been replaced by tarmac with kerbstones and a proper pavement. Street furniture such as the electric concrete streetlamp, speed restriction sign and white centre road lines have been added.

30.   Old Linslade, about 1910, showing the canal and railway with road bridge over the line and footpath down to the canal. Today the stile and telegraph poles have gone and the towpath and footpath to the road are covered with weeds. The railway bridge arches have been altered to accommodate today's fast trains. The railway had to go through Jackdaw Hill (Tunnel Hill). This consisted of hard ironstone. It was reported that two firms went bankrupt and several lives lost as a result of having to drill through this solid rock.

31.   War Memorial, Linslade with policeman standing ready to direct the traffic, 1930s. The Bedford Arms hotel is on the right. Due to ever-increasing traffic the memorial was moved in 1955 to the Mentmore Road Memorial Gardens. Traffic was still causing problems at this junction in 1985 when an articulated lorry hit some bollards causing its tyres to burst. Tudor King's newsagents shop was damaged.

Market Cross

The Market Cross is believed to date from the early 15th century. It has a pentagonal-shaped base with seven steps and a central shaft rising to a height of 27 feet. It has two storeys, the upper one containing five figures in niches. These figures are Christ, the Madonna and child, a bishop (possibly St Hugh), a king and St John.

32. This sketch of the Market Cross was drawn by W. Alexander, FSA and published in London in 1803. The southern aspect of the cross is shown. To the left above the archway is a woman looking out of the window of the Eagle and Child inn, which was built in 1640. This occupied the position of Nos 1–5 Market Square and was a coaching inn until 1852 when it was turned into a shop and private house.

About 1650 the cross was 'in such a ruinous state that it greatly endangered the lives of those persons who were passing near it'. It was repaired with the help of a four pence tax levied on the townspeople. Over the succeeding centuries it has been repaired several times.

During the 17th century it is likely the cross was used by the 'swarms of illiterate preachers who existed at that time', as it forms a focal point of the town and is an ideal place from which to speak. Another use could have been the publication of marriage banns as records show they were often publicized on market days.

In 1751 a crowd of people gathered at the cross and pronounced Jane Massey and Catherine Hankes to be witches. The crowd proceeded to make their way to Luton where they intended to 'float' them in the river. Fortunately, a couple of local gentlemen intervened and persuaded the crowd to release their victims.

In the 20th century the cross has been used for several public functions, notably the Proclamation of the Accession of King Edward VII and also George V. More modern uses today include the Christmas carol concert.

33.   Early 1900s view showing the water pump which was used for filling water carts and cleaning the street. The cross, which has been here since the 15th century, provides a focal point for the townspeople.

34.   For over 600 years the cross has provided a meeting place for the people of the town. For example in 1751 a group of townsfolk gathered here and pronounced Jane Massey and Catherine Hankes to be witches. In this 1920s picture children are sitting on the steps surrounded by market traders selling their wares.

35. This 1880s view clearly shows two of the five figures, the crowned virgin and child and the bishop. During the 1852 restoration the five stone figures were removed and placed around the Town Hall. Replicas were carved and erected in their place. Railings were put up to protect the monument, at a cost of £75 borne by Col H. K. Hanmer and John Dollin Bassett.

36. This picture was taken in 1969. The cross was again restored in 1900 under the direction of Mr Bodley, the cost being met by the Town Lands' Trustees. The old figures were substituted for the modern imitations. The stonework was made good and the railings removed. These cast iron railings were used to form the entrance to Page's Park.

Markets and Fairs

The first market held in Leighton is believed to date from the 10th century. It was held on a Sunday morning until the 15th century when it was changed to a Tuesday. Saturday markets were added in the 19th century. *Kelly's Directory*, 1910, states that the market on Tuesday is for the sale of corn, cattle, provisions and other merchandise while the general market on Saturday is for meat, fish and vegetables.

Market tolls were payable to the lord of the manor. Every Tuesday, in the first part of this century, the lord of the manor, Squire Mills, used to position his men at the entrance to Market Square and the High Street. They would collect tolls from the local stallholders and the farmers bringing their animals into Leighton to sell at the market.

There were at least six different fairs held throughout the year. Two of them were St Paul's Fair and Cherry Fair (St Swithin's Fair) which were held on the 25 January and 15 July respectively. From 1752 the calendars were changed and these old fairs were held 11 days after the original grants. An order dated 22 August 1905 states that they are to be held on Tuesdays after the original dates.

The Horse Fair, which was originally granted in 1447, was held in the week of Whit Tuesday in Lake Street. The turnover of horses was once given as 4,000 for this three-day fair.

The Statute Fair or 'Statty' as it was known was held on the first Tuesday after 11 October. Men and young girls would stand on the south side of Market Square waiting to be hired by farmers. Shepherds would wear a piece of wool in their lapels, cowmen wore cowhair, while grooms would display a piece of whipcord. They would receive one shilling for their day's trouble and in addition the men had a pint of beer. The hire period was for one year for wages of £12 per annum in the early 1800s. The fair was last held in 1896.

The Wool Fair, which originated about 1840, was held on the first Friday of July. Farmers would bring their fleeces to be auctioned at the fair which was held in Church Square. During the two-day fair as many as 70,000 fleeces would be sold. The fair, which was the largest in the county, was last held in the 1920s.

The Fatstock Fair, which is still held today, originated in the late 19th century and is held on the second Tuesday in December.

37. *A conjurer amuses a crowd, early 1900s. Every Tuesday when the market was held, farmers and ordinary people from the surrounding area used to flock into town to buy and sell goods, to hear the latest news and exchange gossip. The pubs were open from 6 am to midnight for the local visitors and workers. No wonder it was known as 'Tiddly Tuesday'.*

38.   *A magnificent view of market day, 1890s, taken by local photographer W. F. Piggott. The High Street is alive with activity. Flocks of sheep in pens are along the sides of the road while horses and cattle are in the background.*

39.   *This scene was taken about 1905. The railings around the Market Cross have gone and a water pump has been installed. A coach with horses is waiting outside the* Swan Hotel.

40.   *Pictured above, about 1890, is the High Street on market day, looking towards the cross from the upstairs window of The Cedars. The sale of animals in the street continued until the 1930s.*

41.   *Pictured is a similar view taken some 74 years later by Bedfordshire County Council photographer K. Whitbread. The livestock has been replaced by market stalls occupying both sides of the street. Sandwiched between them is the traffic.*

Churches and Chapels

From whichever direction one approaches Leighton the spire of All Saints Church dominates the scene. This beautiful old church built in the 13th century has survived several misfortunes, the most recent being in 1985 when the church was ravaged by fire causing a million pounds worth of damage. Restoration work is expected to take several years to complete.

Another church even older than All Saints is St Mary's Church, Old Linslade, which dates back to the 12th century. Unfortunately, this church is only open on special occasions as the parish population has moved to Linslade where the church of St Barnabas provides for their needs.

In recent times with the freedom from religious intolerance many nonconformist churches or meeting places have been set up. It is interesting to note that in 1775 seven men who were appalled by the low moral standards in Leighton set about forming the Baptist Church, the first nonconformist church in the town. It is not known where the first services were held but in 1776 Robert Hawkins, a friend of the minister Joseph James, started negotiations to buy a small chapel and house in Leck End now known as Lake Street. Baptisms were performed in the river Ouzel.

Rev James' successor was the Rev Thomas Wake from Kent. When the Rev Wake went to preach in the surrounding villages he was provided with 'a horse, a large macintosh with four or five capes, a pistol and a whip'.

In 1937 the church hit the headlines over three marriages which took place there which were illegal. Apparently these marriages were celebrated in 1934 and 1935 without the attendance of the registrar and because of this the marriages were technically invalid. In order to validate the marriages it was necessary for a special bill, known as the 'Marriages Provisional Order Bill' to be drawn up for submission to the House of Commons.

42. All Saints Church is believed to have been built on the site of a wooden Saxon church. It is thought the building of the present church began in 1220. The building was finished in 1288. It is built mainly of local sandstone and stone from nearby Totternhoe. The tower carries a broach spire of oolitic limestone which is 191 feet high. This drawing was made in 1862 by John Sunman Austin, a Bedford architect.

43.　Interior of All Saints Church. Pictured is the nave with the altar in the background, early 1900s. The wooden lectern, in the shape of a golden eagle with outspread
wings, dating from the 13th century, can be seen in the background. This is still in use
today and the original chain used to secure the bible to the lectern is still present.

44.　View about 1920 showing the sanctuary with the east window in the background.
Note the gas lamps on the right. Electricity did not arrive in Leighton until 1926.

45.   *Rev and Mrs T. W. Richards and two other ladies sitting in the church garden, 1890s.*
Thomas Wallis Richards, MA was rector of All Saints for 38 years from 1862 to 1900.

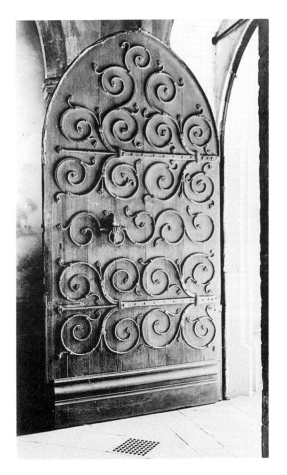

46. *West door of All Saints Church. The door itself is modern but still has the original ironwork and hinges which were cast in the 13th century. The ironwork is attributed to Master Thomas of Leighton, who was commissioned about 1293 to make the wrought iron grill for the tomb of Queen Eleanor in Westminster Abbey.*

47. *In the north-west corner of the south transept one can find this late medieval graffiti, dating from about 1400. The tale goes that it represents two poor local people, Simon and Nelly, who decided to prepare a special Sunday dish for a visit home by their children on Mothering Sunday. They decided to make a cake with a little dough and a piece of Christmas pudding. The dough was put around the cake but they could not decide whether to cook or boil it. In the graffiti Nelly can be seen holding one of her wooden spoons while her other hand is clutching Simon's ear. Happily they eventually compromised and first boiled the cake and then baked it. This is supposed to be the origin of the first simnel (Sim-Nel) cake.*

48. The former Primitive Methodist Chapel, North Street, 1905. Built in 1890 at a cost of £2,340 this building could seat 500 people.

49. Lake Street Baptist Chapel was built in 1864 on the site of the previous chapel. It was reported that when the first pastor arrived in Leighton in 1775 the 'moral state of the town was deplorable, with bull-baiting and cockfighting abounding'. The chapel was built in the Italian style, it cost £900 and was capable of seating 500 people. It closed in 1972 and was demolished some 11 years later. Private houses have now been built on what was the graveyard and chapel.

50. *Wesleyan Chapel, Hockliffe Street. The foundation stone of this £5,000 church was laid in July 1864 by Sir Francis Lycett, Bart. It has now been demolished and today the site has been rebuilt and is occupied by Energy House. The chapel seated 1,200 people but this number was often exceeded on special occasions. In the basement was a large schoolroom, library and additional classrooms, all of which were used on a Sunday. On either side of the chapel were houses appropriately named 'Wesley Villas' which were built for the ministers. One of these buildings still remains and is today used as a veterinary surgery called 'Ark House'.*

51. *Baptist Chapel, Hockliffe Street. Built in 1892 at a cost of £4,000 this chapel could seat 670 adults. A school was also built adjacent to the chapel. This Baptist group was formed in 1832 as a result of a split with the Lake Street church due to dissatisfaction with the pastor and with their open communion policy.*

52–53. *Friends Meeting House, exterior and interior views, 1969. Land was acquired in 1789 for a proper building for the local Quakers. The Friends Meeting House as it became known, was built near to the Black Horse in North Street. It was extended in later years and the Quakers still meet here. Although many Quakers prospered through trade they could not indulge in ostentation or undue luxury without violating their faith. The tombstones at the rear of the building are very plain and identical in size, in keeping with their belief that all men are equal.*

54–55.   *St Andrew's Church, 1905, cost £3,805 to build and was consecrated on 11 July 1867. The church which was similar to its mother church, All Saints, had a spire 110 feet high. The church was built in North End Lane now called St Andrews Street and it could seat 600 people. Unfortunately poor quality sandstone was used from a local quarry in Church Street which resulted in the church having to close in 1964. In 1969 the former vicar, Rev John Scammell said: 'The stone is so soft that birds have pecked right through the wall.' The church has now been demolished and houses built on the site. However, the lych-gate seen in the picture still remains.*

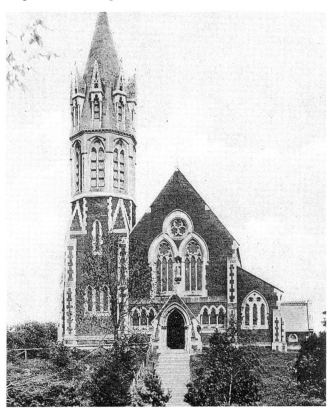

56. *St Mary's Church, Old Linslade pictured in 1911. The nave and chancel were built in the early 12th century. The west tower was built in the middle of the 15th century. About 200 yards to the north of the church, where the Grand Union Canal runs, was a 'holy well', the chalybeate waters of which had a widespread renown for miraculous healing. In 1299 the Bishop of Lincoln prohibited pilgrimages to the well. Anyone defying the ban was to be excommunicated.*

57. *Pictured in 1985 is the damage caused by swarms of wasps to the reddish sandstone tower. Over 300 individual stones are affected. The holes are made by the wasps living and breeding in the church walls. The church is now open only on special occasions as regular services are no longer held.*

Proposed Erection of an additional CHURCH, and a SCHOOL for the education of the Poor, in the Parish of Linslade, Bucks.

The Committee appointed for the purpose of carrying the above design into execution, earnestly solicit the attention of the Public to the following statement.

The number of the Inhabitants has been ascertained to be 869, by far the greater part of which has sprung up within the last four years.

The establishment of the Leighton Railway Station, which, with the extensive Building Ground adjoining, is in the centre of Linslade Parish, having been the cause of the late extraordinary increase of the population, affords the strongest assurance that it will continue to advance at a rate equally rapid.

The Church is not capable of containing more than 150 persons, it stands at a distance varying between one and two miles from the Houses of nearly the whole of the Parishioners, and a mile and a half from that district where the great augmentation in their number is expected to take place.

There is no School in the Parish for the education of the Poor, and the distance of the Church prevents the establishment of even a Sunday School there with any prospect of success.

It is proposed to build a New Church, and a School near at hand, in the heart of the population.

Estimates have been taken and the expenses have been laid at £1900.

Without further appeal to the Christian feeling of the Public, the Committee venture to hope that a simple statement of these facts will induce the religious of all classes whom it may reach, to come forward liberally to the relief of so large a number of their brethren labouring under a spiritual destitution rarely equalled in this Country.

Linslade, June 16, 1840.

N. B. Subscriptions are received at Messrs. Bassett, Grant, and Bassett's Bank, and at the London and County Joint Stock Bank, Leighton Buzzard.

The following Subscriptions have been raised in the Parish and its immediate Neighbourhood, no further application having been hitherto made.

The Rev. B. Perkins, *Incumbent of the Parish*,	£ 25	0 0
The Rev. Henry Matthew, *Curate*,	£ 25	0 0
John Osborn, *Churchwarden*,	£ 25	0 0
Thomas Purrett, *Churchwarden*,	£ 25	0 0
Mr. William Cotching, *Linslade*,	£ 25	0 0
Mr. John Peeby, *Ditto*,	£ 10	0 0
George Adams, M. A. *Ditto*,	£ 5	0 0
Mr. Ridgway, *Ditto*,	£ 5	0 0
Mr. William Brown, *Ditto*,	£ 2	0 0
Edward Lawford, Esq. *Leighton Buzzard*,	£ 50	0 0
Arthur Ashfield, Esq. *Ditto*,	£ 10	0 0
Rev. S. F. Cumberlege, *Curate of Ditto*,	£ 5	0 0
Rev. H. Foulis, *Rector of Great Brickhill*,	£ 50	0 0

58. *Handbill printed 16 June 1840 to 'induce the religious of all classes whom it may reach, to come forward liberally to the relief of so large a number of their brethren labouring under a spiritual destitution rarely equalled in this country'. The result of this appeal by the Rev Perkins, to raise money to build the church of St Barnabas, amounted to only £240. The matter was held in abeyance until 1847 when a more successful attempt was made to raise the finance.*

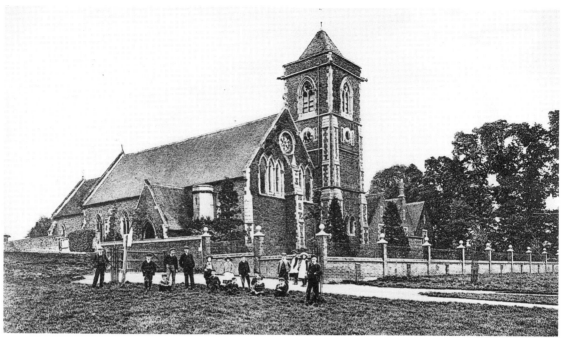

59. *St Barnabas Church, Linslade, about 1904. The church, together with a school, was built in 1849 after a more successful appeal by the then incumbent Rev Ouvry. The land for the buildings was given by Dr Edward Lawford. The church cost over £2,600 to build and the school nearly £1,000.*

60. *Interior of the church, decorated for the Harvest Festival, about 1904. The gas lighting was originally installed in 1862. The cost was £38 16s 0d for floor-mounted gas standards.*

61. *St Michaels and All Angels Church, Grove, before its conversion into a private house in 1972. The building measured only 29 feet 6 inches long, 18 feet wide and about 40 feet high. It is now known as 'The Old Church House' and a sign on the front wall reads: 'This building, once the smallest in Bucks, served a small hamlet which lay in the field across the lane. Probably of Norman origin, it was rebuilt in the 14th century and partly restored in 1883. It was made redundant in 1971 and sold by the Church Commissioners in the following year for conversion into a private dwelling house. The bell dated 1676 has been taken to Westonbirt, Gloucestershire, and the Norman font to Llantrisant, Anglesey.'*

Schools and Education

The earliest reference to education in Leighton is the inscription in the chancel floor of All Saints Church to one Edward Hargrave, MA, who died in 1707. He is described as a gentleman of York, curate of Linslade, rector of Fleet Marston and master of Leighton School for 52 years.

In 1710, Joshua Pulford, who was vicar of Leighton from 1673 to 1710, bequeathed property in his will, the income of which was to be used for teaching children of the inhabitants of Leighton.

The 'Pulford School Room' was built in 1790 and was the gift of the Hon Mrs Leigh. In 1884 this school was sold to the Post Office and a new school built near the recreation ground. In 1872 the St Andrew's School was built at a cost of £1,400.

Boys and girls were educated at both schools until 1893 when education became free. In that year Pulford School became the Anglican school for boys and St Andrew's the Anglican school for girls.

In 1813, local Quakers Dollin Bassett and John Grant helped to found and build the British School (Lancastrian School) in Leighton on the corner of Windmill Lane and Newman Street (Beaudesert and East Street). The school was for the children of parents who were nonconformists and who did not wish their children to go to an Anglican school. The building consisted of one room, to which an additional classroom was later added.

The Lancastrian Method was adopted at this school. The method was based on a system devised by Andrew Bell, which was subsequently improved and developed by Joseph Lancaster. Joseph Lancaster, a British-born educator, claimed to be able to educate a thousand children at a time by using some of the pupils as monitors. The ten brightest children would first be taught to read. These would then be used as monitors to teach another ten children, who in turn would eventually teach another group. The schoolmaster would go from one group to another, offering encouragement or reprimanding where necessary. During the early 19th century this system as developed by Joseph Lancaster, Andrew Bell and Jean-Baptiste Girard and was widely used to provide a rudimentary education for children in Europe and North America.

In one corner of the Lanky-Dee School, as it became known, on a platform some three feet high was the master's desk. From here he had a clear view of the classroom. When not visiting the small groups the master would instruct the senior boys in mathematics or handwriting. Flourishes and ornamentation played a large part in the art of writing.

On the far side of the room, running the whole length, were two long, shallow boxes raised above the floor. They were six inches wide and two inches deep and filled with sand. Alongside these boxes stood the small boys. A monitor would draw a letter in the sand with his finger and then at his command, the little fingers of the small boys would try and copy his example. The results would be inspected and the boys standing to attention would wait for the order to 'smooth sand'. When the small boys had mastered the sand they were promoted to the slate division and eventually had the honour of a writing book.

The various groups in the room would be engaged in reading, writing and arithmetic. In the afternoon the bible would be read and explained by the schoolmaster. Religious instruction was an important part of the school curriculum. In the rules issued in 1840 to parents the following was stated: 'It is requested that every parent will hear their children repeat every morning and evening the prayers which they will be taught at the school; and it is urged on them as a solemn duty to enforce upon their children by their own instruction and example the good lessons taught at school – to read the Scriptures and worship God, with their children, to keep the Sabbath day, to attend public worship, and to walk in all things according to the faith and practice of true Christians.'

Occasionally pupils had to be punished. One punishment was for them to be placed in a wicker cage. This consisted of a wicker basket which was suspended from two hooks on the underside of a large cross beam, some ten feet from the floor. The basket was narrow which meant that the child had to stand in the basket. This form of punishment was used up until 1870. If the basket did not cure the pupil he was placed in the cupboard below the master's desk. In the darkness it was hoped that the child would realise the foolishness of his ways.

Cedars School was founded in 1921. The building was once the home of the Harris family, who were part of the firm Basset Son and Harris, bankers. The school was situated at the lower end of the High Street and was formed in response to requests from the local people for a secondary school in the town so that their children would not have to travel to neighbouring towns for their schooling.

The school grew from 106 pupils in 1921 to nearly 400 by 1945. Entry was by means of examination and interview at the age of 11 and pupils were drawn from a very wide area. After 1965 the idea of abolishing selective schools and replacing them with comprehensive schools prevailed. Bedfordshire adopted a three-tier system of education with lower, middle and upper schools. Cedars School was to become an upper school catering for children aged 13 or over. In order to accommodate 1,100 pupils it became necessary to build a new school on the Mentmore Road playing-field site. Building took place between 1972 and 1979.

62.   *Leighton High School and Kindergarten, November 1926. Lawn tennis is being played but the group of four girls sitting on the ground look as though they have been playing croquet.*

63–64.   *Taken between the two World Wars these pictures show the front and rear view of Cedars School when it was situated at the end of the High Street. John Dollin Bassett, a local banker, had the house built in 1858 and called it 'The Cedars'. The house became a secondary school for boys and girls in May 1921. It opened with 106 pupils, 42 boys and 64 girls aged between 11 and 16. The old school is now Leighton Middle School and caters for children aged 10 to 13.*

65–66. *1930s pictures of Cedars School cookery class and swimming pool taken by Arthur J. Anderson. Transport to school during the 1920s and 1930s was not easy. Many pupils had to walk several miles to and from school, some even rode on horseback, stabling their horses at the* Ewe and Lamb *in Bridge Street.*

67. *The Forster Institute, 1985, 1 Waterloo Road. This adult school was built in 1890 in order to educate the local working men. In 1962 the building was described as containing two large rooms, with the upper room having a raised stage (the Barron Knights played here in 1960). The downstairs room, once used for billiards, was mentioned as being used as a headquarters for the First Linslade Girl Guides.*

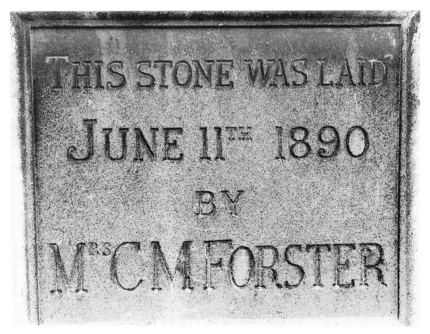

68. *The stone commemoration plaque, which was laid by Mrs Forster, is to the left of the entrance.*

69.   The British School, which had been founded by the Quakers in 1813. When the Board School was built, the original building became an infants school. It was altered and enlarged in 1894 to accommodate 300 children and became known as the Beaudesert Infants School.

70.   A school board was formed in 1893 by the trustees of the Church and British Schools, so that they would be eligible for money from public funds. The board's first project was the Board School, Beaudesert, built in 1894. The school was enlarged in 1900 to accommodate 330 pupils (boys). It subsequently became known as the Beaudesert School.

71–84. The following four pages of photographs appeared in the booklet Centenary Celebrations of Leighton Buzzard British School *published in 1913.*

The headmaster of the Beaudesert School at this time was William Sinclair Currie, who was appointed head at the age of 23, the youngest headmaster ever to be appointed in Bedfordshire. He retired in 1929. The school had an excellent scholastic record and in 1919 it was recorded that applications for school places far exceeded the number available.

Photo]   [Anderson.
MR. JOHN DOLLIN BASSETT.
Founder.

71

Photo]   [Anderson.
MR. THEODORE HARRIS.
Secretary and Manager for 30 years.

72

Photo]   [Anderson
MR. DAVID COOK.
Pupil 1853-8.

73

Photo]   [Elliott & Fry.
ROBERT TINDALL, ESQ., J.P.
Manager, Secretary, &c., for 30 years.

74

MR. JABEZ INWARDS.
Headmaster — to 1847.

75

Photo] *[Maull & Fox.*
MR. E. W. LEWIS, F.R.G.S.
Headmaster 1861–81.

76

Photo] *[Wyles.*
MR. G. H. MAJOR, F.C.S.
Headmaster 1881–86.

77

Photo] *[Anderson.*
MR. W. S. CURRIE.
The Present Headmaster.

78

E. J. WILKS, ESQ., J.P., F.R.G.S.
Pupil 1860–62.

79

H. BROWN, ESQ., M.P.
Pupil 1866–76.

80

REV. W. ABRAHAM, M.A., D.D.
Pupil 1857–66.

81

MR. HENRY SELL.
Pupil 1859–62.

82

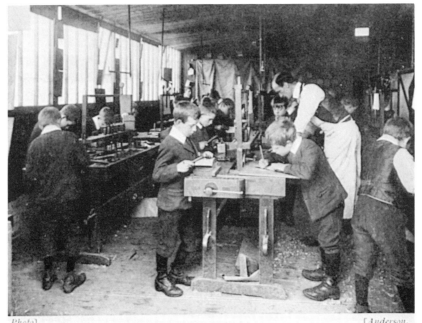

BEAUDESERT COUNCIL SCHOOL WORKSHOP.

83

CRICKET TEAM.

84

Local Characters and Groups

We know of one local figure from the past, Captain John Salusbury, from a diary he kept. He lived in the 18th century and his diary covers the years 1757–1759.

Captain Salusbury was an educated gentleman and lived a very comfortable existence. He held public office including Justice of the Peace and lived in 'a fair sized house near the centre of the town'. He took advantage of its location by letting his railings to horse traders on market days. He had a well-stocked garden and orchard which provided him with food throughout the year, and belonged to a local club called the Civic Society, which met in local pubs, and whose members came from many walks of life 'such as grocers, tailors, carpenters and even an attorney'. He does make reference though, to the harsher realities of life in Leighton Buzzard for the not so fortunate. On 20 August 1757, 'Judge Foster, at the town assizes convicted four prisoners for horse and sheep stealing and two for burglary. They will be hung as is the custom.'

More recently, Leighton resident Tom Lawson recalls some of the local characters he knew as a young boy.

'Boss' Brookes lived alone in a big ramshackle house opposite Heath Pond on the corner of Shenley Road. He had a boat on the pond and for a copper or two would take you for a trip.

Charlie King lived by his wits collecting bits and pieces with his donkey and cart. He liked his pint as most people did in those days and his donkey was no exception. It was very comical to see it having a drink.

'Happy' French was a man who had terribly misshapen feet. Often he could be seen pushing a pram full of odds and ends that he had collected. He regularly did the job of nightwatchman minding a hole in the road. 'Happy' used to sit in his hut with a large brazier burning while he cooked his meal, usually a rabbit, on a shovel. Although a rough and ready character his house was spotless.

'Punch' Miles had an eyelid that dropped so he had to look up to see you. He did odd jobs like tarring water barrels all for just a few coppers to buy a pint of beer.

Poaching rabbits before the war was a very popular pastime. Many local men were involved including 'Blood' Major, who worked at the abattoir. His wife would go out with her pram round the houses selling the night's catch for 6d each.

During the war when food was short people found ways of supplementing their rations. Bernard Smith from Aylesbury recalls that near the Leighton railway station there used to be a labyrinth of rabbit holes in the embankment. It was not uncommon to find passing goods trains slowing down near this spot. The fireman would then throw lumps of coal at the rabbits. Any direct hits were recorded by the driver blowing the train's whistle. The guard would then jump from the train and pick up the stunned rabbit.

Other Leighton characters included 'Wryneck' Alice, an extremely tall woman who walked with her head on one side; 'Snuffy' Kempster who kept a barbers shop in North Street and 'Jilliper' Abrahams, who when in the army, was reputed to have told the officer in charge of a route march that as they were walking a bit too fast he would 'just tag along behind'.

85.   *Alderman Sir George Woodman, JP, pupil 1856–57, Beaudesert Council School (Leighton British School). In 1904 he was knighted and made Sheriff of London. He was a director of the London and Commercial Bank.*

86. *John Stairs, town crier, continuing in the family tradition, 1910.* Kelly's Directory *of the same year lists him as being a town crier and butcher, 14 North Street.*

87. *Mr Gotzheim, organ-grinder.*

88. *Fred Rowe, first scoutmaster.*

89. *Rev Charles Edward Douglas, BA, who started Leighton Buzzard scouts and founded Faith Press, which printed religious books, Christmas cards, church pamphlets and articles. He was curate at All Saints and is reported to have invented the stamp for Sunday School attendance. Rev Douglas died in 1938 but Faith Press continued until 1979.*

90.   *1st Leighton Boy Scout Troop, July 1912, by the Market Cross. Included in uniform are Jack Butcher, Fred Rowe, Caleb Smith, F. Brotherton, Fred Groom and W. Quick.*

91.   *Orchestra, pictured outside the Baptist Chapel, Lake Street, about 1913. In the picture are Mr and Mrs Tom Bunker and their daughter Barbara.*

92. *Faith Press works outing to Bletchley Park, 1913.*

93. *Salvation Army Band 19 May 1916. Back row: J. Harvey, A. Aris, C. Gaskin, H. Marks, A. Quick, H. Quick, W. Green, E. Weller. Front row: H. Tyler, Capt Covarrs, F. Fox.*

94.   A well-known local football team, the Ivy Leaf Reserves, playing in the Ascott League in the 1920s. James Eastaff is holding the football. Also in the line-up are: Jack Tompkins, Harry Lake, Fred Biley, Harry Hopkins, Fred Short, Arthur Evans, William Brandom, F. Kemster and Ben Hyde.

95.   A line-up of local bathing beauties, pictured after their swim in Spinney Pool, about 1929.

96.   Outing of the Leighton and Linslade Tradesmen Association to Thames Valley, about 1930. Included in the picture are: Leonard Croxford, Mr Skevington, Mr Hopkins, Sam Dillamore, Bill Summerfield, Mr Barnet and Mr Allder.

97.   The Leighton Buzzard Home Guard. This consisted of local men who trained in the evenings. They learnt how to defend the town in the event of an invasion by the Germans.

98. *23 Platoon, E Company, 6th Battalion Beds Home Guard.*

Back row: Pte Ansell, Pte Willis, Pte A. Evans, Pte King, Pte Rendell, Pte O. H. Roberts.
4th Row: Pte Parsons, Pte Forsyth, Pte Watkins, Pte Tooth, Pte Boyle, Pte Clarke, Pte Foster.
Pte Lancaster, L/Cpl Anderson, Pte Thomas, Pte Horn, Pte Harper, Pte Scrivener, Pte W. J. Evans, L/Cpl Crowther, Pte Lathwell,
Pte B. Biley, Pte Fleckney, Pte Harvey, Pte Gubbins.
3rd Row: Pte Lake, Pte F. Biley, Pte Janes, MM, Pte Lancaster, L/Cpl Anderson, Pte Thomas, Pte Horn, Pte Harper, Pte Scrivener, Pte W. J. Evans, L/Cpl Crowther, Pte Lathwell,
2nd Row: Pte Hayes, Pte Birdsey, Pte Underwood, Pte Richendoller, Pte Dew, L/Cpl Murdock, L/Cpl Gibbins, L/Cpl Yirrell, L/Cpl Holmes, L/Cpl Dickens, L/Cpl H. A. Rollings,
Pte Jeffcoate, Pte Linnell, Pte G. Roberts, Pte Baines, Pte Challoner, Pte Heckford.
Front Row: L/Cpl Turner, L/Cpl Woolhead, Cpl Sewell, Cpl Meeking, Sgt King, Sgt George, Sgt Hyde, Sgt Graham, Lt Tooley, Major Croxford, MM, 2nd/Lt Rush, 2nd Lt Clifford,
Mr E. F. Plummer, JP, Sgt North, Sgt Pantling, Cpl Cook, Cpl Pimm, L/Cpl Underwood, L/Cpl Short.

99. *VE street celebrations, May 1945. Represented are people from Wing Road, Mentmore Road, Ashburnham Crescent and Leighton Road.*

100. *Party for the old residents of Leighton held in what is now the Bossard Hall, about 1948. The men in the white coats are local butchers.*

101. *Wesleyan Infant Sunday School Class, about 1949, taken at the Wesleyan Chapel in Hockliffe Street.*

102. *Third annual picnic party of the Leighton Twins Club, held August 1984 at Parsons Close Recreation Ground. Seven sets of twins and two singletons can be seen. The twins are: Nadia and Rosanna Marrone (with sister Bianca), Claudia and Nicola Millburn, Helen and Lisa Bacon, Catherine and Joanna Wedgeberry, Amy and Lucy Hince, Barnaby and Alexander Goddard, Richard and Timothy Phillips.*

Historic Buildings

There are lots of fine, interesting buildings in Leighton Buzzard. Many originated in the Victorian era, though there are a few dating back to earlier times such as the *Black Horse* inn which dates from the 17th century and the 'Hearth and Home' premises which go back to the 15th century. The town suffered two calamities which destroyed much of the earlier buildings. The first was during the Civil War when Royalists plundered the town and the second was during a disastrous fire in 1645.

A feature of the town is the number of 18th-century houses faced with local bricks. These were handmade from clay dug in the area and fired in kilns using a local heather called ling. The bricks have a patchy, blue glazed finish.

One of Leighton's more interesting buildings, Leighton House, survived until the 1950s. It was believed to have had a mysterious secret tunnel which led to a cellar in the church-yard of All Saints Church.

In 1950 a member of an old Leighton family, Miss Constance Wagstaff, recalled that her father Dr Philip Wagstaff, who died in 1894, was one of a party who actually entered the tunnel when a bricked-up doorway in the house was opened. The tunnel was later sealed. Miss Wagstaff was told by her father that the passage led to a cellar in the churchyard. This cellar, the last remnant of the ancient Prebendal House, was sealed in 1949 because it was unsafe.

Another Leighton resident, Mrs G. Smith, saw the tunnel in 1897 when her husband worked as a footman at Leighton House. Apparently he once showed her the entrance to the tunnel to which he had a key.

The cellar in the churchyard is reputed to have been used by choirboys as the scene for initiation of new members. The ceremony consisted of being pushed into the dark damp vault, popularly known as the 'Devil's Grave'.

Just before Leighton House was demolished in 1958, Vivian Willis of the Leighton building firm R. Willis and Son, visited the cellars of the house but could find no evidence of any tunnel.

103.   Sketch of Market Square in 1793 showing the old timbered Market Toll House. The bell was used to call townspeople to hear announcements and attend meetings by the Market Cross.

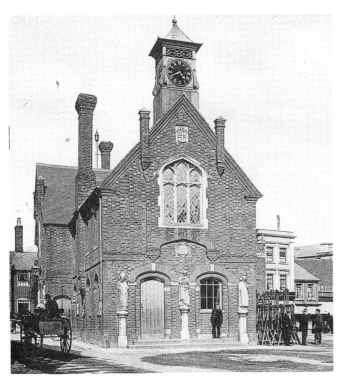

104. The old Market Toll House was replaced by this building in 1851 at a cost of £1,182 which was paid for by the lord of the manor. Originally, the upper storey was used as a Town Hall (the County Court was held here), whilst the open ground floor was used by market traders. At the beginning of the century the ground floor was filled in and was used to store equipment and stalls. From 1919 it was used as a fire station until a new one was built in 1963. Today the upper floor is a club for the British Legion with the ground floor being used as a council store and a rest room for old people. The latter is run by the WRVS.

105. 1950s front view of the old Town Hall and fire station. The council purchased the market rights and Town Hall from the lord of the manor, J. T. Mills, in 1918 for £1,200. One of the conditions of the sale was that the hall and rights should be for ever retained by the council for the use of the town. Leighton at this time possessed several public clocks. The opportunity was taken by the council to overhaul the Town Hall clock and adjust it to Greenwich each day from a signal received at the post office. This resolved what had been a 'standard source of irritation' as all the public clocks tended to differ.

106.   Council Offices 1962, which have now been demolished and replaced by a car park. The premises were built in the 19th century for the Leighton Buzzard Working Men's Mutual Improvement Society. In 1889 the premises were described by H. Jackson as 'a fine reading room, library, recreation room and Biblical library, also a dwelling house for manager and a well appointed kitchen from which cooked food is supplied to invalids'. In 1891 the upper floors were taken over by the newly formed Leighton Buzzard UDC to be used as council offices. This building in North Street was known as The Institute and it was here that the Evening Secondary School was held.

107.   Built in the second half of the 19th century this attractive building known as the White House, was originally a private house. It was purchased by the Leighton Buzzard Urban District Council in 1962 for £15,000. Today the building houses the South Bedfordshire District Council's finance division. In 1985 the question of it being a listed building was discussed at a local council meeting. According to the Department of the Environment the building is of insufficient interest to become a listed building.

108. Leighton House was situated at 28 High Street. Baron Ferdinand de Rothschild used it in 1875 as a town house. In the 1920s the ground floor was converted into two shops while the upper floor was used as office premises. In 1958 the whole building was demolished and is now occupied by the Co-operative furniture store.

109. The old bricked-up doorway adjoining Leighton House. It was said to be the remains of a Cistercian house once a cell to Woburn Abbey. The doorway is in the Renaissance style and is probably mid 16th century. Tradition says that this cell contained an underground passage which led to the precinct of the church. It was demolished in 1958.

110.   *Early 1900s view of the Post Office with telegraph boys in uniform waiting near the front entrance. This building was taken over in 1884 by the Post Office which moved from 5 High Street. Prior to this the building had been used as a school and was known as the 'Pulford School Room'. The Church built a new school in Parsons Close, still keeping the name Pulford.*

111.   *Modern picture of the Post Office. The exterior remains the same except for the gas light. The main entrance is now on the left-hand side of the building as 7 Church Square, occupied by J. J. Clarke, painter and decorator, was pulled down in 1950.*

112–113. The largest block of granite ever quarried in the British Isles was used in 1920 to commemorate the 171 Leighton men who were killed in the 1914–18 war. The block was obtained from the Shap quarries. The monolith stands in Church Square and is 25ft 3in high by 3ft 3in square. It weighs 22 tons and took 3 days to erect. Lord Ampthill unveiled the war memorial on 11 November 1920 in front of a crowd of 5,000 people. One picture shows the memorial as it was in 1920 whilst the other shows the epitaph and names of the men who fell in the 1939–45 war.

114.   Sketch by J. Lawford, about 1850, of the old vicarage which stood in Church Square.

115.   Post-war view of 24 Lake Street known as 'Lake House'. This 17th century building was thought by Robert Richmond to have been originally a tavern known as the Maiden's Head. During the Second World War the house was occupied by the army. It was pulled down in 1956 to make way for the new telephone exchange.

116–117.   Two opposing views of the Corn Exchange showing what this elegant building was like before and after the removal of the spire in 1932. This building was built in
1862 on the site of the George public house and cost £7,500. An exquisite Bath-stone
portico stood over the pavement and the spire rose to 85 feet. Inside the building there was
a large assembly room, several meeting rooms and a theatre. The building was demolished in the 1960s.

118.   *Leighton Buzzard library, now Lecton House, pictured in 1978 with Lake Street Baptist Church (left). Originally the building was a temperance hall. It was built in 1845 and financed by two local Quakers. The hall served as an adult education centre for morally uplifting instruction.*

119.   *The new library, which is called the Library and Arts Centre, stands on the opposite side of Lake Street. It was opened in October 1979 by Lord Miles of Blackfriars.*

120.   Page's Almshouses, Church Street, about 1905. These six almshouses were built in 1903 from a request in the will of Councillor William Sharp Page, a pawnbroker. He also gave the town a field now known as Page's Park. The almshouses cost £1,200 and were built on the site of the sandstone pit which had been dug for the construction of St Andrew's Church.

121.   Almshouses, North Street. The original buildings were built by Edward Wilkes in 1630 in memory of his father John. The almshouses were rebuilt in 1857 and extended in 1873. They provide accommodation for ten poor widows. Edward's son Matthew, who was a London ironmonger, bequeathed funds in his will for an annual commemoration of Rogation Monday. The reading of his father's will still takes place here.

122.   Holly Lodge stood on the corner of North Street and West Street. It was built in 1607 and used as a home until 1936 when the occupant, Miss B. C. Hopwood, who wrote thrillers under the name of Patrick Leyton, moved to Toddington. During the war it was requisitioned and housed evacuees. The house was never lived in again and was finally used as a store by the Leighton Co-operative Society. The building is pictured in 1958 shortly before it was demolished to allow for the widening of West Street. An unusual story about the building states that it was raffled in the 1920s. Some people say tickets were only 1s but others recall them being sold for 2s 6d or 5s.

123.   Former Union Workhouse, Grovebury Road, 1980. The original workhouse was situated in Workhouse Lane (Baker Street). In 1834 Parliament passed the Poor Law Amendment Act. This enabled several parishes around Leighton Buzzard to join together in order to construct a new workhouse. The new building provided accommodation for 100 men, 100 women and 60 children, as well as the workhouse master. It was known as the 'Union'. The tramps would bed down for the night in the workhouse and get up at dawn to break stones in order to earn their keep before moving on to another workhouse at Luton or Bedford. During the Second World War the building was used as a health centre. The building was later turned into offices and is now known as Ridgeway Court.

124.   *This 100 foot high water tower was built in 1896 on high ground in Stanbridge Road (opposite Marley Tiles). The water was stored in two tanks housed in the tower. In the* Official Guide to Leighton Buzzard *published about 1910 it states: 'The council are the owners of the waterworks and provide a constant supply of pure and wholesome water, which is provided free of cost for domestic purposes. The water is obtained from a well over 200 feet deep, bored into the lower greensand, and is capable of yielding a supply of 164,000 gallons per day. The latest analysis made by an eminent public analyst states that the water is "simply perfect" and "is excellent water for public supply".' The tower was demolished in the 1950s.*

125.   *The Southcourt Stud Farm was built in 1880 for Lord Rothschild, who kept his stud of racing sires and brood mares here.*

126.   Leighton Buzzard windmill, about 1820. Windmills are thought to have been introduced into England by the Crusaders returning from the Holy Land. It is recorded that in 1212 at Leighton Buzzard the lord of the manor 'set up a (wind)mill and charged excessive toll for grinding the peoples grain'.

127.   This flowerbed was originally a Victorian horse trough, one of three erected to commemorate the Diamond Jubilee of Queen Victoria. Dogs could drink from the special trough in the base. This trough still stands in Leighton Road although the other two, which were situated in North Street and Golden Square, were removed in 1951.

128–129.   The Martins, built about 1810, stood about half-a-mile north of Leighton canal bridge. It was a magnificent timber-framed mansion modelled on the lines of an oriental pagoda. An ice-house, which was used for preserving ice, stood in the garden. There was also a boathouse. Both pictures were taken about 1905, when the house was occupied by canal engineer, Gordon Thomas. The canal bridge has since been removed. The property was destroyed by fire in the 1950s and today several private houses occupy the site, although the name still exists.

130.   Entrance to Picket Lodge (right), about 1920, at the junction of Old Linslade Road, Plantation Road and Brickhill Road, Rushmere House is on the left.

131.   Today the Lodge has been pulled down and replaced by two smaller lodges.

132–133.   *Ascott House, fountain and gardens pictured in 1904 when it was the seat of Leopold de Rothschild. The half-timbered house was built mainly in the second-half of the 19th century and incorporates a farmhouse built in the reign of James I. It houses the Ascott collection which includes paintings by Reynolds, Stubbs and Turner, fine Chippendale furniture and exquisite porcelain. The collection together with the house, the grounds of 261 acres and an endowment were given in 1949 to the National Trust by the late Anthony de Rothschild.*

Shops and Businesses

There are many shops and businesses in Leighton that provide a service to the local community. Some like the Yirrell's butchers have been in business for generations.

Four generations of this family have run a butchers business in Linslade. The business was originally established in 1883 by William Yirrell who bought premises in Old Road for £910.

The business is now run by another William Yirrell and his son Peter. William Yirrell's father also named William took over the business in 1910. He worked part-time from the age of seven and full-time from 14. He remembers the war years when local families were rationed to 10d of meat and twopennyworth of corned beef a week.

William also remembers what it was like before freezers existed. He recently told a reporter: 'It was cold, very cold. The whole of the front of the shop was open during the winter and summer. The health of the meat was more important than the feelings of human beings.'

In the 1960s the family expanded into farming so they could produce the meat that they sell in their shops which are now in Old Road and the High Street. Today a lot of their meat and poultry comes from their farm in Soulbury, Dollar Farm. They also supply meat to local hotels and restaurants.

In 1914 a 14-year-old schoolboy by the name of R. J. Jackson started work for the first time at the solicitors office of Pettit, Walton and Co, in Bridge Street. Fifty years later he was still at work but the company had become E. T. Ray and Co with offices in Church Square.

Mr Jackson, now chief clerk, recalled his early memories to a *Leighton Buzzard Observer* reporter. 'Mr Walton said he would take me on for a month's trial to see how I shaped – and I did not think for a moment that this would be for the greater part of my life.'

In 1917 Mr Jackson joined the army and served in France and Germany returning to the firm in 1920.

'Working conditions were vastly different from those of today (1964). All correspondence and deeds were written by hand and I was taught the now almost forgotten art of texting with a quill pen while perched on a high stool. Copies of letters were taken off in a screw press. It was not until about 1920 that the typewriter became the usual method of copying and engrossing. All this is in contrast to the present electric typewriter and mechanised accounts system.'

One of Mr Jackson's early duties was to stand in the street outside the office holding the horses of clients while they were visiting the office. On one occasion Mr Jackson nearly lost a favoured client. The customer came from the office protesting loudly that his steed was nowhere in sight. 'I had been holding the wrong horse!' explained Mr Jackson.

134.	Turn of the century view of Deeley's grocers and post office situated at 73 Hock-
liffe Street.

135.	C. Linney and Son, 13–15 Lake Street. This lovely old shop was built about 1876
and still survives today with its horse sign and twin lanterns inscribed 'Linney saddlers
and harness makers'. The horse fair was held in Lake Street. This accounts for the wide
pavement which was where the horses were tethered to the railings.

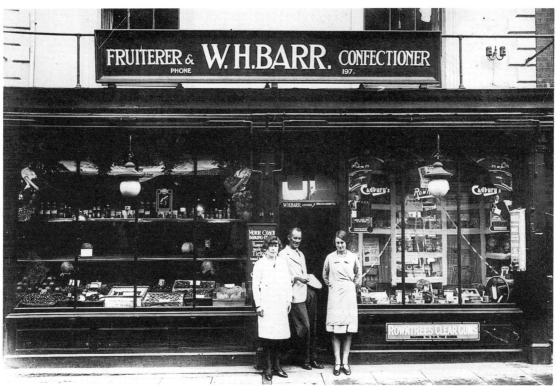

136.   *W. H. Barr, fruiterer and confectioner, 29 Market Square, 1930s.*

137.   *W.H. Baumbrough, grocer and seed merchant, 26 Market Square, about 1910. In those days the shop-assistant was there to offer service. It was his job to pander to the whims of customers, who were of course always right.*

138. *Francis Charles Capel, provisions dealer, 70 North Street, about 1910. The picture was taken by Bert Blinco, a local photographer. It was just before Christmas, judging by the number of turkeys hanging outside the shop.*

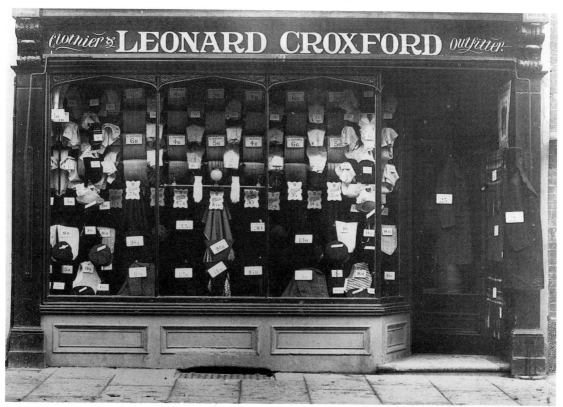

139. *Leonard Croxford, 44 North Street, clothier and outfitter. This 1928 picture shows trousers priced 5s 6d and coats for 25s.*

140. *Percy Wright Oates, butcher and poulterer's shop, 26 High Street, 1906.*

141. *The first petrol station in Leighton was situated at 26 High Street. The original garage was started by Leonard London and known as London and Brown Ltd and was taken over by Frank Webb in the late 1920s. It remained a garage until 1960. Picture taken about 1950.*

142.   *H. Jackson and Co, 5 High Street, printers of the* Leighton Buzzard Observer
and North Bucks Times *with Anderson the photographer next door at No 7. Alexander
Muddiman founded the* Leighton Buzzard Observer and Linslade Gazette *in 1861.*

143.   *The grocers, Home and Colonial Stores
Ltd, 49 High Street, selling 2lb bags of sugar
for 1s 3d. The clock was installed by Frederick
Taylor, watchmaker and jeweller, who was a
previous owner.*

144. *George F. Green's ironmongers shop, 32 High Street, with Mr Fletcher (manager) standing outside. Notice the sign above the door advertising the Ingersoll 5s watch.*

145. *J. H. Green and Co, corn, seed, cake and forage merchants, maltsters and hop factors, 34–36 High Street, about 1907. Outside the shop stands a horse and cart laden with sacks. The notice outside the shop advertises the Leighton Buzzard and Linslade Traders Exhibition to be held on Friday and Saturday November 26th and 27th.*

146. *Greens Stores and Sketchley Cleaners, 1962.*

147. *The London Joint City and Midland Bank Ltd, which arrived in 1920 and built new premises on the site of 48–50 High Street, the former home of Gibbs and Co, house furnishers. On 27 November 1923 the name of the bank changed to Midland Bank Limited. In those days banks did not employ any women staff because 'we felt they could not keep a secret'. Today banks could not run without women and if they all walked out the business world would soon grind to a halt.*

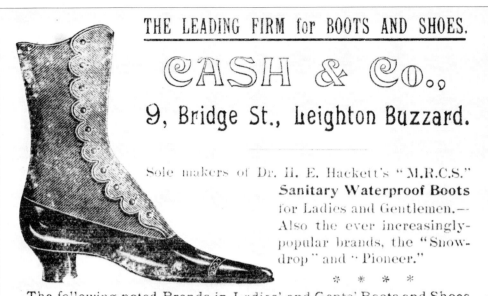

THE LEADING FIRM for BOOTS AND SHOES.

CASH & Co.,
9, Bridge St., Leighton Buzzard.

Sole makers of Dr. H. E. Hackett's "M.R.C.S."
Sanitary Waterproof Boots
for Ladies and Gentlemen.—
Also the ever increasingly-
popular brands, the "Snow-
drop" and "Pioneer."

* * * *

The following noted Brands in Ladies' and Gents' Boots and Shoes
are also kept in stock:—"The Waukerz," "The City," "Oceanic,"
"Walkalong," "Faultless," "College," "Crossover," "Citizen,"
"Acme," "Gazelle," "Louis IX."; also Vienna and Paris makes.

*Sole Agents in the district for the celebrated "Elasta" Shoes, fitted with a
patent pneumatic pad.*

N.B.—Cash and Co. make Boots and Shoes to measure. Their bespoke department
receives special attention. **Repairs a Speciality.**

148.   Advert for Cash and Co, boot and shoe manufacturers, 9 Bridge Street, 1905.

*149.   George Monson's brewery, Wing Road, about 1909. The brewery was only here
for a short time, the building was later occupied by Faith Press. It is now the home of
Motor Vehicle Services.*

Hotels and Inns

The early inns or taverns were identified by simple signs such as lions, swans or horses. Many of these old inns had gardens or bowling greens and some even had their own brew houses for making beer.

The three main coaching firms in the town during the 17th century were the *Eagle and Child* (1–5 Market Square) the *Swan* and the *Unicorn*. They provided accommodation and refreshment to the coach travellers who used to rest here while on their way to London or the university towns of Cambridge and Oxford.

During the 18th century many local houses became public houses. Their customers were the farmers and local residents who used to flock into the town on market day. The ale houses used to stay open all hours as licensing regulations as we know them today were not brought in until the First World War.

Beer was brewed in the town. Ashdown Brothers' brewery, part of which is now occupied by the Bossard Shopping Centre, was well known in the 19th century. Their ale, stout and porter was much liked by the local community. With the coming of the tied-house system the business declined and Benskins of Watford took over at the turn of the century. Part of the brewery was demolished in 1920 when Walter Pratt, agricultural engineer, bought the Brew House at 15 High Street.

The following list of beer retailers, taverns, public houses, commercial inns and malsters is taken from Slater's Directory of 1850:

Inns – Commercial etc

Elephant & Castle (and posting), Henry Richardson, Linslade
Swan (& posting), John Bushell, High Street
Unicorn, Charles Claridge, Leek Street
White Horse, Jno Heckford, Hockliffe

Maltsters

Clarke, Jeremy, North Street
Franklin, Henry, Leek Street
Loke, Charles, North Street
Reeve, Charles, High Street
Sell & Claridge, Leek Street
Warner, John, Canal Street

Taverns & Public Houses

Bedford Arms, Thos Gurney, Canal Wharf
Bell, Thomas Ginger, Market Place
Bell, Charles Inwards, Hockliffe
Bell & Woolpack, Thos Tompkins, Leek Street
Black Horse, Sarah Birdsey, North Street
Black Lion, Thomas King, High Street
Boot, Charlotte Gandy, Market Place
Buckingham Arms, Austin Horwood, Linslade
Bull, John Deverell, High Street
Bull, John Inwards, Hockliffe
Coach & Horses, Thomas Parsons, Leek Street
Cross Keys, Richard Samuel, Market Place
Curriers' Arms, Ann Marlton, Market Place
Duke's Head, William Tompkins, Heath and Reach
Ewe, Lamb & Shepherd, William Loke, Canal Street
Falcon, George King, Leek Street
Five Bells, Joseph Eames, Standridge

Fleur-de-Lis, Richard Tompkins, Hockliffe
George & Dragon, Henry Franklin, Leek Street
Golden Bell, Ann Cotching, Church Square
Greyhound, Thomas Barker, North Street
Horse Shoes, Wm Lancaster, Egginton
King's Arms, Wm Inwards, Hockliffe
King's Arms, Rd Irving Buyers, North Street
Nag's Head, James Snoxell, Leek Street
Peacock, Thomas Gilbert, Leek Street
Peacock, Jos Powell, Heath and Reach
Plough, William Pantling, Egginton
Plume of Feathers, Geo Young, Leek Street
Railway Inn, William Ebbern, Linslade
Raven, Elizabeth Dickins, High Street
Red Lion, Robt Belgrove, Heath and Reach
Red Lion, Joseph Scott, Standridge
Roebuck, John Garside, Jeffs Lane
Royal Oak, James Payne, Back Lane
Saracen's Head, Charles Loke, High Street
Shoulder of Mutton, Jas Turney, Canal Street
Star, Thomas Hickson, Heath and Reach
Sun, John Young, Leek Street
Swan, Edward Secret, Chelsea
Wheatsheaf, Thomas Sanders, North Street
White Hart, John Green, Hockliffe
White Swan, Richard Woods, Hockliffe

Retailers of Beer

Barker, William, Hockliffe Road
Bunker, Joel, Hockliffe
Cook, David, Back Lane
Fall, Thomas, Chelsea
Faulkner, William, Linslade
Hitchman, Joseph, Linslade
Holt, Benjamin, Standridge
Honour, William, North Street
Hopkins, Joseph, Back Lane
Mead, William, Linslade
Milles, John, Linslade
Norman, Joseph, Hockliffe Road
Reeve, Thomas, Heath and Reach
Samuel Thomas, North Street
Smith, William, North Street

Although public houses were traditionally owned and operated by licensed publicans by the early 1900s many pubs were owned or otherwise connected to a small number of brewery companies.

Over the last two hundred years the number of pubs has declined rapidly despite a rapid rise in population. In the early 1800s there were 64 hostelries in the town but by 1930 the number had declined to 42 even though the population had quadrupled to 9,500. In 1980 when the population had reached 30,000 there were only 29 public houses remaining. It is interesting to note that only one new pub, the *Clay Pipe*, has been built in Leighton Buzzard this century. This pub is situated in Appenine Way and was built in 1978. It derived its name from the clay pipes found on the site.

LINSLADE,

LEIGHTON BUZZARD, BEDS.,

Close to the Station, on the London and North-Western Railway, which is within an hour's ride from London.

Particulars and Conditions of Sale

Of all that much-frequented and valuable Freehold Property known as the

"RAILWAY HOTEL,"

Adjoining Church Street, and occupying a most eligible site, facing the Railway Station,
having every convenience for carrying on a lucrative trade, with

GROOM'S COTTAGE, AND LOOSE BOXES FOR 9 HORSES, &c.,

enclosing a

LARGE YARD.

ALSO A MOST ELIGIBLE AND COMMANDING

RANGE OF BUILDINGS,

Now used as 13 LOOSE BOXES, with Loft over part of the same, and extensive

COACH-BUILDING PREMISES,

WITH A FRONTAGE OF 136 FEET TO THE CHURCH ROAD.

WHICH WILL BE SOLD BY AUCTION, BY

MESSRS

HART & SONS,

At the Assembly Rooms, Corn Exchange, Leighton Buzzard,
On *Thursday, March 5th, 1863,* at 4 for 5 o'Clock punctually,

BY ORDER OF THE MORTGAGEES.

PARTICULARS AND CONDITIONS OF SALE may be obtained of Messrs. WATSON & SONS, Solicitors, Bouverie Street,
London; at Muddiman's Printing Offices, Leighton Buzzard and Aylesbury; and at the Auctioneers' Offices'
Leighton Buzzard, Ascott, and Burcott.

150.   *Poster advertising the sale by auction of the* Railway Hotel *on 5 March 1863. By 1881 the hotel had changed its name to the* Hunt Hotel. *It once had stabling for 100 horses and was the centre of the local hunting fraternity. London gentry would arrive by train and change their clothes at the hotel, returning after the hunt for poached eggs in the dining room. In 1923 the last Prince of Wales rode from the hotel but unfortunately had to be treated by local physician, Dr Square, when he broke his shoulder blade in a fall near Little Billington. An express train heading towards London was stopped in order to transport the prince home.*

151. The Black Horse, *1985, corner of North Street and West Street. It is believed to be the third oldest building in the town and may well have been an alehouse from the 17th century. It was largely rebuilt during the 18th century.*

152. The Plume of Feathers *hotel, 11 Lake Street, was situated next to the Corn Exchange. The person chatting in the light suit is Lawrence Inns who started the Lawrence Inns Band. The hotel was demolished at the same time as the Corn Exchange in 1968.*

153. Swan Hotel, *1905, which started life as a drinking parlour in the 17th century but because of the position of the town (on the main road between Oxford and Cambridge) it soon developed into a coaching inn or posting house. Two coaches left daily, one to Oxford and one to Cambridge. Prints dating from the 17th century show the hotel as a low two-storey building with bow fronted windows. The building has since been altered and the façade seen above is believed to date from the middle of the 18th century. The name of 'Bushell' printed in the centre of the building refers to the Bushell family who owned the hotel from 1805 until the First World War. The hotel was refurbished in 1981 and now has 35 bedrooms all with bath, colour television and telephone.*

154. *Interior of the hotel, 1952. Some of the people at the bar include Charlie Woods (bottom left), Mr Roberts the local bookmaker (left), and Sam Bunker (right).*

155.   The White Lion, *North Street, with Florence Webb standing in the doorway.*

156.   The Peacock Inn *was situated at 1 Lake Street. The building dates from the 15th century and is the oldest Leighton Buzzard business still standing. The narrow front is due to the fact that frontage space was valuable. The building extends back for some distance from Peacock Alley. In 1979 it was converted into a shop, and is today occupied by Hearth and Home.*

157.   *This photograph of the* Globe Inn *was published by Francis Frith (1822–98) who was one of the great pioneer photographers of the Victorian era. Frith and his assistants travelled widely and captured thousands of views on glass plates. His pictures were sold in tobacconists and grocers shops throughout the land and their popularity helped persuade the Post Office to accept the picture postcard as a form of postal communication. The* Globe Inn *was erected prior to the coming of the canal even though this passes within a few yards of its front door. The inn is believed to be 17th century and is situated on the old packhorse track from Leighton to Old Linslade.*

158.   *The* Unicorn Hotel, *Lake Street. This inn was built about 1638 and had a priests hole with a passageway that wound from one floor to another. This 1907 picture was taken when James Stevens was the proprietor. Printed on the postcard are the words: 'Family and commercial hotel with loose boxes for hunters, situated in the centre of Lord Rothschilds, the Whaddon Chase and Hertfordshire hunts. Also good accommodation for motorists, cyclists and pleasure parties. Shooting, cricket etc and lunches catered for.' In the early 1970s it was turned into a nightclub.*

Industry and Work

Leighton Buzzard grew up as a market town relying on the surrounding farmland for produce and livestock sales. It developed further through business connected with the local sandpits. This accelerated when the Grand Union Canal was built in 1800. A thriving haulage and transport industry grew up to deal with the increased demand for sand. The railway came in 1838 and brought closer contact with London and the North. This made Leighton an attractive site for various businesses and as a residential area for commuters, which in turn helped local businesses.

JOSEPH ARNOLD AND SON'S was founded in the 1870s and still remains a family concern. Peter Arnold, great-great-grandson of the company's founder, is their managing director. The company owns more than 500 acres of land and has six quarries in operation, producing sand for iron, water filtration, asphalting, construction and horticulture. The firm exports to many European countries, Nigeria and other African countries.

GEORGE GARSIDE (SAND) LTD have been established for over 80 years. The building sands division produces sand for the manufacture of roofing tiles, mortars and readymix concrete. The other division, industrial sands, is one of the UK's largest suppliers of sand for water and sewage treatment. The sand used for filtration is over 98 per cent silica, as this does not break up under accumulation of water. The sand is the purest in the world and it is even exported to the Middle East desert states.

GOSSARD LTD opened a factory in Grovebury Road in 1926 to manufacture large quantities of laced-back corsets which were fashionable at the time. During the 1939–45 war they switched to manufacturing large parachutes and also smaller ones which were used for Very Light Flares. In the 1950s the company began designing bras and today it is one of the leading bra manufacturers with export sales to many countries. The firm employs several hundred people.

LIPTON EXPORT LTD moved to premises in Stanbridge Road in 1974. The founder of the firm was Sir Thomas Lipton who started with a small provisions shop in Glasgow in 1871. Today the company in Leighton provides work for 700 people who blend and package tea and teabags. The factory produces around, 2,000 million teabags each year and export their famous Yellow Label tea to over 120 countries. Their major markets are Scandinavia, the Middle East and the Far East. In 1979 they were granted the Queen's Award for Industry in recognition of their export achievements.

LANCER BOSS, Britain's biggest lift truck exporter, was started in 1957 by two brothers, Neville and Trevor Bowman-Shaw. The company moved to Grovebury Road in the 1960s and has now become Leighton's biggest employer. Being a leader in the field of sidelift handling, the company offer the world's largest range of frontlift, sidelift and container handling lift-trucks. Some 70 per cent of total sales are exported to around 120 countries and the company boasts several Queen's Awards for export achievement. The company is still privately owned and has an annual turnover in excess of £70m.

CAMDEN MOTORS started in 1946 in Soulbury Road where they renovated and sold used cars. The premises consisted of two large sheds and a van body, which was used as an office. In 1947 the Lake Street premises were opened with the Soulbury Road site being used for paint spraying and repair work until 1961 when the site was closed and new premises opened in Grovebury Road. Today the company is one of the largest car sale companies in Britain.

The MARLEY TILE CO LTD came to the town in 1926 and grew from a small factory in a field to become by 1939 the biggest producer of concrete roof tiles in the world. Another tile factory, REDLAND TILES LTD of Grovebury Road was originally called the Leighton Buzzard Tile Co and became part of the Redland Holdings group in 1962.

Local building firm WILLIS DAWSON LTD began as two small family firms which merged in the 1960s. Other industry in Leighton includes: GRUNDFOS PUMPS LTD, established in 1964, which manufactures various types of pumps; ROSEWEAR who export clothing and AUSTIN BEECH LTD an engineering company. A totally different activity in the form of tourism was introduced by WYVERN SHIPPING CO who offer a variety of boats for hire on the Grand Union Canal.

162. A Leig
Northern Dist
womenfolk an
people. They

159.   Advert for town gas, 1910. The gas-works were situated in Union Street (Grovebury Road) near the Leighton to Linslade branch railway line. This enabled coal trucks
to be brought to the works direct from the coalmines.

163. Bar
(right). Th
capable of
sand at O
wich, near

160. Thr
from the st
ing the she
of the thre:
The jackst

164. *Brantoms Wharf, Linslade 1928. The barge belonged to Harvey Taylor, canal carrier from Aylesbury and is seen here loading wheat for delivery to London. The two gentlemen on the right are A. Holmes and A. Barton. The wharf and bridge have since been filled in.*

161.
blacks

165. *Turn of the century picture of Gilbert's foundry, Mill Road where the work of casting in iron and brass was carried out as well as milling and engineering work. The firm later moved to St Andrew's Street where they still carry on the engineering and milling trade.*

166.   Staff and workforce at Morgan's coachbuilders, 1923. Most of the employees are named here: works manager, Ezra Reeve; body shop foreman, Arthur Faulkner; panel shop foreman, Richard Hayes; trimming shop foreman, Charlie Ridgeway; finishing shop foreman, Fred Underwood; paint shop foreman, Mr Turton; saw mill foreman, Jack Shirley; engineering shop foreman, George Dixon and chief electrician, Mr Maynard.

The other workers are: Giles and Harry King, Jack Parker, Tom Bunker, William Sharrett, Ernest and Cyril Stevens, Tommy Tooms, Sidney King, Bill Thornton, Jack Lancaster, Joe Compton, Joe Chandler, Charles Kidell, Frank Faulkner, Tom Sanders, Bill Haythorne, Sam and Frank Smith, Walter Chamberlain, Jack Brotherton, Ezra Hasley, Sid Field, Albert Willis, Frank Roe, Horace Jeeves, Sid Cheshire, Dick Chamberlin, Mr Felce, Wally Luck, William Botsford, Jack Horn, Arthur Burchell, Sidney Tyas, Dick Hopkins, Jock Hallwood, Anna Prudent, Charlie Rimmington, Arthur Evans, Tony Rimmington, Wally Whitney, Horace Whitney, Sam Everett, Charlie Stevens, Ena, Joe and Bassey Mills, George Jennings, Sidney Wakefield, George Goodman, Jack Darville, Ernest Thorpe, George Roberts, Fred Woodman, Ernest Hillsdon, Mr Griggs, Frank Heckford, Fred Bonham, Percy Green, Fred Chandler, Charlie Shepherd, Sidney Fletcher, Fred Evans, Mr Thompson, Charlie Brown, Frank Edwins, Ralph Toyer, Ernest Fathers, Tom Underwood, Bill Higgins, Percy Brinklow, Fred Green, Mr Pratt, Mr Richardson, Horace Woods, Arthur Bunyan, Jimmy Rice, Jack Holland, Mr Childs, Mr Worsley, Frank Gibbs, Bernard Hayes and T. Terney.

The four apprentices, pictured at the front are: Evan Brown, Bill Tooms, Leslie Blake and Albert Hopkins.

167.   The trimming shop at Morgans, 1923. The chassis were imported from America and the cars finished here. Customers would often sit on a wooden frame to test what sort of cushion they needed for maximum comfort. The car cushion could then take as long as a week to finish as everything was done by hand. Workers usually worked from 7.30 am to 7 pm from Monday to Friday for a basic wage of £4 a week plus bonuses.

168. *Local fire brigade pumping water from flooded cellars of residences in the district, 21 May 1924. Three violent storms in three days caused the worst floods, the heaviest losses and damage since the great cloudburst of 1879. The Ouzel began to rise quickly after the storm and within half an hour had covered Lake Street. Several other streets were soon waterlogged and the town was completely isolated by water.*

169. *Sandpit workers or 'sand-dobbers', Mr Reeves and Mr Lee, about 1925. Until the 1930s sand quarrying was mainly done by hand. Workers were paid six shillings a day.*

170. *Early locos, about 1920, Billington Road. The Leighton Buzzard Light Railway Company was formed in 1919 to carry sand from the pits in Vandyke Road to the Billington Road sidings of the L and NW railway. This had become necessary as the sand-carts were destroying the local roads. In 1917 for example, Grovebury Road cost as much as Bedford High Street to maintain.*

171. *Fire Brigade, 1920. P. D. Payne was the captain with W. J. Pratt as superintendent of the 10 men in the brigade. Their equipment consisted of two manual engines together with a mile-long hose!*

172.   Fire Brigade, 1940, outside the old fire station in Market Square.

173.   Auxiliary Fire Service, 1939. The voluntary part-time AFS provided a back-up
to the main fire service during the Second World War.

Leisure and Recreation

Leighton Buzzard offers a wide variety of activities in the form of clubs and societies of which there are over 200. These range from the Children's Book Club to the War Games Club. There are also many interesting places to visit nearby, such as Ascott House or Whipsnade Zoo.

Closer to home are parks and recreation areas, most noteably the modern leisure complex at Tiddenfoot and its waterside park. At the leisure centre one can take part in keep fit, gymnastics, life-saving, yoga, karate, tennis, swimming, squash, roller-skating, cricket, hockey or just relax in a spa bath or sauna. The waterside park consists of 30 acres and offers the opportunity to go fishing, jogging, walking or pony trekking and is ideal for picnics.

Life in Leighton Buzzard has not always been so congenial as local resident Tom Lawson recalls. Before the war people had very little leisure time and very little money to enjoy it. Holidays were a day at the seaside or a bicycle ride and birthdays, Easter and Christmas were the highlights of the year.

Christmas in the 1920s was a very special time especially for children who were more naive then, and thought of it as magical and mysterious. It was also the only other time apart from their birthdays when the would receive any sort of presents.

Money was hard to come by for most people but without the pressures of modern day advertising on television and radio (of which there was neither) expectations were lower and people were generally happy with very simple pleasures.

There was only one main toyshop and toys were very different. A clockwork Hornby train was a real treat. More common were marbles, spinning-tops, hoops, cricket bats and balls, footballs and the cards from cigarette packets and these all had their own special season.

Christmas dinner was the highlight of the year with chicken as the main course. It would only be eaten about twice a year, quite different from nowadays. Then came the Christmas pudding with its 3d pieces inside, and what a scramble to get them!

People made their own amusements, as there was no electricity there were no televisions, video games or other gadgets in the home. There was generally one gas light and then candles. You would carry a candle up to bed with you or try to keep one alight while you walked down the garden to the toilet. It wasn't until the late 1940s that Tom Lawson remembers being in a house with an inside toilet and bath.

Children amused themselves by running or biking to local areas such as Totternhoe. There was very little traffic on the roads, a car was something to stop and look at. There were plenty of horses however, and the children could follow them with a 'truck' and shovel and earn themselves a halfpenny or a penny. A penny a week was the usual pocket-money for a child so shopping around was essential. Jordon who made his own sweets in Victoria Street was the best buy, you could get a bag of sweet dust for a penny and this could be pressed together to make one big sweet.

It cost a penny to go to the pictures and very often you were given a comic or an orange on your way out. They were silent pictures but the cheering and shouting by the audience made up for this. A piano usually accompanied the film and when the 'Four Horsemen' was shown Fred Groom did the trumpet calls and everyone thought it was wonderful. If you went at night you usually had to queue or book a seat.

Another popular entertainment was watching flying displays at Billington Road, especially if you could afford a flight. It was very exciting watching planes fly at 90 miles an hour!

A favourite of the children in the summer was the Walls 'stop me and buy one' ice cream man on his three-wheel bike, or Ben Olney with his barrow of home-made ice cream. There were other interesting people to look forward to, Johnny the Italian and his barrel organ and the rag-and-bone man with his barrow. If you gave him some rags or a rabbit skin he would give you a penny, a windmill or even a goldfish. Simple things now but they meant a lot in those days.

The floods were another regular visitor, as soon as it rained hard or there was a thunderstorm you took out your floodboards to cover the doorways. This happened several times a year and would still occur if the rivers were neglected.

Holidays were very simple, a day at the seaside with the Sunday School or a trip on the canal to Linslade in a cleaned out sand or coal barge. There the children would run about, have some cake and lemonade and then return on the barge to Leighton Buzzard. A treat to be remembered was a ride to Luton on the bus, then a ride on the trams and a visit to Woolworths, where nothing cost more than sixpence. The annual outing for the cubs was on Good Friday when they would meet at the hut with their food and drink and then set off on a walk to Ivinghoe Beacon. There they would play about all day and then walk all the way back. A special trip Tom Lawson remembers was when he went with Mr Roberts and his family to Ashridge on a horse and dray. They all piled aboard but had to get off at steep hills to lighten the load and sometimes they had to help the horse by pushing!

174–175.   In 1891 Leighton Urban District Council was formed. One of its first acts was to purchase from the Church Commissioners the ground seen (above). This was to provide a recreation area known today as Parsons Close. An architect, Mr Gotto was engaged to design the layout which resulted in trees being planted, paths laid and shrubberies created. Pictured (above) is the recreation ground in 1918. Houses have been built in Church Avenue in the 1985 view (below). Today this 8.78 acre site boasts a paddling pool, slides and bandstand.

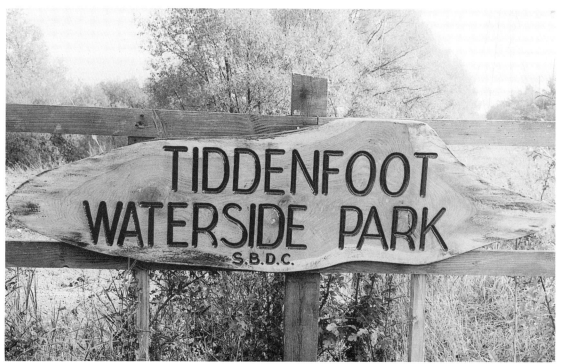

176–177.   *Tiddenfoot Waterside Park is a former sandpit which is now ideal for walks and picnics but unfortunately due to the absence of signs it is difficult to find. The only sign visible is pictured (above) and that is partly obscured from the road by bushes. The 30 acre site is situated next to Cedars Upper School and the small car park is adjacent to the Blackburn Stables on the Mentmore Road. Wooden picnic tables and seats are available and the 8 acre lake provides fishing for members of the local angling club. There is a trim trail, comprising a 400 metre joggers' track with activity stations. There is also a pony trekking trail while a footpath follows the canal to Linslade.*

178.   The thatched boathouse, Stockgrove Country Park, situated on the west bank of the lake. Pictured here as it was, before being destroyed by fire shortly after the Second World War.

179.   This picture shows the foundation and ironwork that remain today.

180. Stockgrove Country Park. This path runs besides the feeder stream which feeds the lake. Baker's Wood is on the right. This wood of approximately 34 acres is a Primary Oak Woodland, which the Nature Conservancy Council has designated as a site of special scientific interest. A particular feature of this wood is the large number of bluebells which appear every year.

181. Part of the ornamental concrete seat next to Stockgrove lake showing the Kroyer Kielberg coat of arms. This seat stands as a memorial to one of the owners of the estate, Michael Kroyer Kielberg, a Danishman. Between 1929 and 1939 he had the house rebuilt and the parkland re-landscaped.

182. *Oriel cinema, Lake Street, about 1935. It was named after the oriel windows of the house of Dr Lawford which stood on the site before the cinema was opened in 1922. The cinema manager used to inspect the staff each day before opening to ensure that they had clean shoes and tidy hair. In the 1960s the decline of the cinema audiences forced it to be converted into a bingo hall. The building was demolished in 1985 and today in its place stands a Kwik Save food store.*

THE Oriel

Western **SOUND** *Electric* **SYSTEM**

'Phone 160.   Leighton Buzzard.

MONDAY, AUGUST 29th, for 3 Days. Matinee on Tuesday at 2.15 p.m.

ROBERT MONTGOMERY in

Lovers Courageous,

With MADGE EVANS.

Frederick Lonsdale's most charming Romance. Also—
LEON M. LION in
"CHIN CHIN CHINAMAN."

The story of a jewel theft and its amazing denouement.

THURSDAY NEXT: CONSTANCE

THURSDAY, SEPT. 1st, for 3 Days. Matinees on Thurs. & Sat. at 2.15 p.m.

TALLULAH BANKHEAD in

"THE CHEAT."

Tallulah gives her best performance to date. 'Also—
Charles Rogers and Peggy Shannon in
"THIS RECKLESS AGE."

A comedy drama of youthful high spirits.
BENNETT in "REPUTATION."

183. Leighton Buzzard Observer *advert for the Oriel, 1932.*

184. *Edwardian view of the St Barnabas Church and recreation ground. The ground was given by Henry Finch, JP. The young saplings in the foreground have today turned into mature horse-chestnut trees.*

185. *This drinking fountain was erected by the aid of public subscription and dedicated on 13 August 1903. Water can be seen gushing from the lions' mouths. Pewter mugs chained to the lions' necks were provided for thirsty visitors to the park. The inscription on the side reads: 'This fountain was erected to commemorate the generosity of Henry Finch, JP of "The Gables", Linslade in making a free gift of this public recreation ground and his many other munificent acts.' Today the drinking cups have gone, the water no longer pours from the lions' mouths and the monument top has disappeared.*

186.   *Bridge Street, with the Grand cinema on the right. This cinema was built in 1922 by Mr Yirrell a local builder. The first manager was G. H. Blackburn and music was provided by Rosie Rowe on the piano accompanied by Richard Anderson on the violin and musical saw. It ceased to be a cinema about 1932 and is now the car showrooms of Dunham and Haines.*

187.   *Lawrence Inns Syncopated Orchestra, which played at the local Corn Exchange during the 1920s, 1930s and Second World War. The band became famous and made radio broadcasts, records and film music.*

LEIGHTON BUZZARD CARNIVAL.

COME AND SEE

THE LATE AN BOOZE ARD
FIRE BRIGADE.

Fires attended after 24 hours notice, and in strict rotation.

DISTANCE NO OBJECT.

When not engaged at fires, we contract for baked Spuds and Chestnut Parties.

Special Terms for School Treats and Slate Club Outings.

"FIREMEN ARE BORN, NOT MADE."

Our men are carefully picked Eskimos, to whom Fire is an anathema.

IF DESIRED WE ATTEND FIRES IN PLAIN VANS.

Send us a Post Card and test our defences.

WINNERS, LEEDON CUP 1815.

The only Fire Brigade to beat Aston Villa on their own ground.

Tel. No. "BURNEM" 1 by 1.
Tel. Address: "HOTSTUFF, HADES."

Bogus Claims Substantiated.   Terms: BEER IN ADVANCE.

IN CASE OF FIRE, CUT ROUND DOTTED LINE.

DON'T FORGET OUR JUMBLE SALE.

IN CASE OF FIRE, CUT ROUND DOTTED LINE.

F. W. Bendy, Printer, Leighton Buzzard.

188. *Handbill advertising the Leighton Buzzard Carnival, printed by F. W. Bendy, 1931.*

189. Postcard published by F. W. Bendy, Bridge Street, of bathing in the sandpits, Billington Road. This was better known as Spinney Pool, and was used by the Leighton Buzzard Swimming Club, which was founded by R. Willis and G. Stockwell in 1921. The pool was 300 yards long, 50 yards wide and up to 40 feet deep. Landing stages, swimming huts and a 36 foot high diving board were built. The ASA held national swimming and diving events here.

190. Members of the 'Barron Knights', well-known pop group from Leighton and Dunstable, who celebrated 25 years in showbusiness in October 1985. Knights Pete Langford, Butch Baker and Dave Ballinger are pictured here in May 1985 sharing an early Silver Jubilee birthday cake with the oldest resident at Westlands Old People's Home, Miss Evelyn Redman, aged 96. Also pictured are Hazel Fletcher and Ivy James.

191. *The first passenger train of the Ironhorse Preservation Society leaving Page's Park, 3 March 1968. The train ran to Double Arches and back making a round trip of seven miles. Note the passengers standing precariously in the open wagons. The four-mile-long line was originally built to serve the sandpits. The idea for the society came from two Hertfordshire model railway enthusiasts, Brian Harris and Laurie Brooks. Later the society was renamed the Leighton Buzzard Narrow Gauge Railway Society.*

192. *'Pixie' (Kerr Stuart 'Wren' Class 4260, 0 – 4 – 0T), built 1922, seen here crossing Hockliffe Road, about 1969. In 1985 the society carried 9,947 passengers. Today the society has over 300 members of whom about 70 actually put in regular voluntary work on the line. Some volunteers are so keen that they travel long distances to help with the railway. Nearly every week in 1985 one tracks expert was travelling from Essex to help.*

193. *The second wireless set in Leighton Buzzard built by Mr Brotherton, pictured 1922. The licence cost 10s, a lot of money in those days.*

LEIGHTON BUZZARD.

A WIRELESS EVENING.—The commodious schoolroom connected with Hockliffe-street Baptist Church was not nearly large enough to accommodate all those who wished to attend the wireless lecture and demonstration held there on Thursday evening. The event was jointly organised by Mr. J. Chapman and Scoutmaster Brotherton, and it is interesting to recall that while wearing the King's uniform they operated wireless signals by Tutankhamen's tomb. Mr. Chapman was responsible for the verbal portion of the evening, and described in simple language the development of the principles underlying the phenomena, through the researches of a number of early pioneers, to the practical utility of the present day, and emphasised how each experimenter had succeeded in obtaining a greater measure of control over the waves. He treated, as far as was possible before an uninitiated audience, of the manner in which the waves are created and launched in space, to spread until too weak to be recorded by the most sensitive instruments, and how those within range were picked up, amplified and translated once more into morse signals, speech, or song. Meanwhile, the waves emanating from the small concert room on the seventh floor of Marconi House were being intercepted by an indoor aerial in the roof of the building, and by the aid of eight sets of telephones attached to long leads, a similar number of the audience, moving along in relays, were able for a few moments to verify the lecturer's assertions. The practical part of the demonstration was in charge of Scoutmaster Brotherton, who, all unaware of the Post Office edict to be issued the next morning forbidding apparatus to be transported from the user's premises, had brought along his very excellent, but largely home-made, set from the scout hut. Some of the members of the audience left at a reasonably early hour, but it was not until eleven o'clock, "Uncle" Burrows announced "2LO closing down. Good-night all," that the more ardent spirits could be persuaded to go home. It needed but few words from the Rev. J. H. Brooksbank to obtain from the listeners-in expression of their warm appreciation of the services of Messrs. Chapman and Brotherton.

194. *A newspaper account of a wireless evening held in a local schoolroom in the 1920s.*

Leighton Buzzard Observer and Linslade Gazette

The founder and proprietor of this local newspaper was Alexander Phillips Muddiman. He was a printer, stationer and fancy goods dealer with a business in the High Street where Boots the Chemists stands today. The first edition contained national news from other papers, the local news being confined to just two columns of the four-page newspaper. By 19 February 1861, less than two months after the first issue, the paper's circulation had reached 1,000 copies.

In August 1865 J. Muddiman senior took over and he was later succeeded by Joseph Muddiman who died aged 75 in 1874. Elizabeth Muddiman then became the proprietress and in 1882 the business was moved to 5 High Street, where new steam-operated printing presses had been installed. The paper passed from the hands of the Muddiman family on 31 March 1885 when Henry Jackson took control.

In 1909 Harry Midgley took over the business and he was succeeded by his son David in 1944. When David Midgley died in 1948 the paper was bought by Home Counties Newspapers. The title was later changed to the *Beds and Bucks Observer*. In July 1986 the paper moved from their offices at 14 High Street to above the DJ Computers shop at 17 Bridge Street.

195.   *First copy of the* Leighton Buzzard Observer and Linslade Gazette *which was issued on Tuesday, 1 January 1861, price 1d unstamped and 2d stamped. The residents were obviously not impressed because in the second issue the editor complained that it had been said 'What did the town want with a newspaper? Things had gone on very quietly; why are they to be disturbed now?' The newspaper survived and is still printed today as the* Beds and Bucks Observer, *price 14p.*

Leighton Buzzard Observer
AND LINSLADE GAZETTE.

Vol. 71. No. 35. TUESDAY, AUGUST 30th, 1932. PRICE TWOPENCE.
Registered at the General Post Office as a Newspaper.

FIFTY YEARS AGO.

EXTRACTS FROM "THE LEIGHTON BUZZARD OBSERVER" OF 1881 AND 1882.

THE ROTHSCHILDS.

In October, 1882, the Rothschilds were the virtual owners of one fifth of the fertile land in the delta of the Nile, and their share in bonds was popularly estimated to be £12,600,000. An envious anti-Semite calculated the income of Baron Wilhelm Rothschild at about £23 per hour, or 9s. per minute.

LEIGHTON STATUTE FAIR.

Leighton Buzzard's annual statute fair with its noise and filth, obstruction and nuisance was held on October, 17th, 1882. The High Street and Church Street were as usual, completely taken possession of by the roughs and rapscallions of the itinerant show and stall society and the crowding and the din almost totally annihilated the business of the ordinary market. Since the purposes for which the original "statty" was originally established have long since been met by other means more in accordance with the requirements of modern civilisation," it was stated, "it is a pity that some step is not taken to relieve the town of this unnecessary and painful infliction."

ARMY DESERTER AT HOCKLIFFE.

MOTOR PATROL'S CAPTURE.

The capture of a deserter by motor patrol was described at Leighton Buzzard Police Court on Monday afternoon.

George Daniel Albert Everley, of Goodjarat Barracks, Colchester, was charged before Mr. Wm. Labrum with deserting from the Royal Fusiliers.

P.c. McCarthy gave evidence that whilst on motor patrol duty with P.c. Turner at 2.30 p.m. in Hockliffe, they saw defendant cycling from London to Nottingham. When they saw that he was wearing grey trunks, they asked him the name of his regiment. He replied: "I belong to no regiment; I have never been in the Army. I tried once to get in but was rejected." Witness asked Everley to take off his coat and waistcoat, and noticed that he was wearing braces bearing a regimental number and "R.F.," which stood for Royal Fusiliers. Although taken into custody he still denied being a deserter from the Army, and gave his home address as Church Road, Hayes, Middlesex. The police there made enquiries, and found that defendant was an absentee from the Army. The bicycle he was riding was his own property.

Supt. R. J. Marritt's request for a remand in custody to await an escort was granted.

In advertising for an assistant Medical Officer for the Bedfordshire Sanatorium, at £386 per annum with board, residence, laundry, garage, etc., and £150 travelling allowance, the Beds County Council says "The salary and emoluments are £100 above the scale recognised by the British Medical Association."

SUNDAY'S STORM.

A heavy storm, which appears to have been quite local, fell in Leighton Buzzard on Sunday evening. For a few minutes rain came down so fast that the eaves' gutterings of houses were unable to carry it away and the water ran down the walls of the buildings. There was also slight flooding through the temporary blocking of drains in Lake Street and Plantation Road. In the latter case two cottages near the Stag Inn had storm water running through the house and sewage forced up out of the yard drains.

195a. Extracts from the local newspaper, 30 August 1932.

LINSLADE URBAN COUNCIL.

A PLAGUE OF CRICKETS.

At a special meeting of the Linslade Urban Council on Tuesday there were present: Mr. W. E. Durrell (Chairman), Messrs. Bell, Dillamore, Faulkner, Labrum, Missenden, Walker and Wing.

The Council considered a complaint received respecting a plague of crickets alleged to emanate from Mr. Allder's herb-drying premises in Soulbury Road.

The Chairman and the Surveyor were asked to meet Mr. Allder to discuss the matter.

The purchase of a four-wheeled refuse van was decided upon.

The Surveyor was instructed to write the County Surveyor about the dangerous position of a lamp standard in Mentmore Road, and to serve notices in respect of hedges overhanging in the footpath from Springfield Road to Leopold Road.

PROPERTY.

FOR SALE.

MR. A. W. MERRY'S ILLNESS.—Mr. A. W. Merry, head of the firm Stafford. Rogers and A. W. Merry, Ltd. who recently underwent a serious operation, has returned home and is going on well.

SHOP WINDOW SMASHED.—A loose stone lying in the roadway in Bridge Street was shot through Mr. W. S. Higgs' shop window on Sunday week, making a small round hole in the plate glass pane.

ALL SAINTS CHURCH.—The Vicar (Rev. G. F. Hills) is returning from his annual holiday and the Rev. E. Scott, who has completed his duties as curate in the parish is spending his holiday motoring in the Pyrenees. He will be away until September 27th.

GUIDES OUTING.—On Saturday the Leighton Buzzard Company of Girl Guides with their Captain, Mrs. Pratt, and Lieutenant Miss Hedges, went by motor coach to Whipsnade Zoo, and spent a very interesting time. They were greatly amused by the bears' tricks and asked the keeper many questions.

LEIGHTON BUZZARD CATTLE MARKET.

A visitor to Cuddington Parish Church heard a continuous scratching sound coming from an old-fashioned stove in the centre of the Church. He opened the stove and out flew a large bird.

195b.   Extracts from the local newspaper, 30 August 1932.

Transport and Travel

The coming of the canal in 1800 meant increased prosperity for the residents of Leighton which in turn led to an increase in population as people were attracted to the town.

The canal was used for the transport of timber, grain and flour from London docks and coal from the Midlands. The town sent them sand in return. Three wharves were constructed to enable the goods to be unloaded and stored. They were called Charity Wharf, Leighton Wharf and Witcheloe's Wharf.

The railway came in 1838 and threatened to replace all other means of conveying goods and passengers. In 1861 the railway timetable published in the *Leighton Buzzard Observer* showed that there were 11 up trains and 12 down trains between Leighton and London. Some of these were fast non-stop trains (first and second class only) taking approximately one hour. The single fares were 7s, 4s 6d and 3s for first, second and third class respectively. The three different classes gave rise to the saying: 'First Class was high caste, Second Class was low caste and the Third Class was outcast.' The canal system survived because although it took longer to transport goods by water it was still cheaper than the railway.

The cheapest way of transport was by road but the conditions of the roads varied considerably. Many sections of the highway had been owned and maintained by turnpike trusts. This system was never popular and in the end parliament refused to extend the licences when they came up for renewal. Parishes were reluctant to keep the road under repair, so it was not until 1875 when the roads were placed under the authority of the district councils by the Public Health Act of 1875, that any regular care was established.

The most common vehicle on the road was the carrier's cart, an open four-wheeled conveyance which used to collect and deliver such things as parcels, sacks, livestock and newspapers. In 1850 for example William Claridge went to London from the *Unicorn* every Tuesday while Timothy Deacon journeyed to Luton on Tuesdays, Thursdays and Saturdays from the *Roebuck*. The carrier would also do your shopping for a small charge.

In 1870 the penny-farthing bike appeared. Being so high it was difficult to ride. However, other kinds of bicycle were developed and in 1885 the 'Rover Safety Bicycle', the forerunner of the modern cycle was invented. This provided a cheap form of transport but was not as quick as the motor car, which gained in popularity during the Edwardian period. Mr Hallett, the workhouse master, had the first car in Leighton which he occasionally used as a taxi. He charged 6d to take you from the Market Cross to the railway station.

During the 1920s the Reliance bus operated by J. H. Pope of Hockliffe became a familiar site in the town. He operated a bus service between Leighton and Luton as well as other routes. Mr Pope was proud of his record of reliability in being able to run his buses under any adverse condition be it snow, fog or hail. Only once in 1927, when there was an extremely heavy snowstorm, did he have to withdraw his bus service.

196. No 5 bus run by the Eastern National Omnibus Company which ran from Leighton to Luton (return fare 1s 9d). Pictured 1920s outside the Bell Inn, *Market Square. Similar buses carried troops to the Western Front during the First World War.*

197. *Early 1900s view of the lower end of the High Street looking towards the Market Cross. A horse and cart or bicycle were the main means of transport for townspeople.*

198. *Leighton's first railway station, built about 1838. When this photograph was taken, by local photographer Archibald James Bacon (between 1920 and 1940), the station would appear to be in the back garden of a house. It was situated several hundred yards north of the present site of the station. The station although in Linslade has always been known as Leighton Buzzard station.*

199. *Picture of Leighton station taken by local photographer Percy Baker, around 1915. Passengers are waiting for a train. Flower beds can be seen on the middle platform and the name Leighton Buzzard is written on the gas lights. A coach is standing (right) on the Dunstable line, which was closed in 1962. The train from Leighton to Dunstable was known as the 'Dunstable Dasher'.*

200. *The station pictured some 70 years later. Steam engines were withdrawn during the 1960s and replaced by diesels. In 1966 the line through Bedfordshire was electrified.*

201.   The Three Locks, Soulbury pictured in the 1950s. The canal was opened 28 May 1800. Horse-drawn barges capable of carrying 30 tons, carried local silica sand to Wolverhampton. The horses were stabled along the canal in places like the Three Locks pub, seen in the background, which was originally built as stables. Motorised boats, as seen in the picture, replaced the horse-drawn barge. Barges stopped carrying freight on a regular basis in 1974. However, in 1985 freight was carried again. As an experiment a load of newsprint was transported from Ellesmere Port to Brentford. Today the canal is used for leisure activities as people take to the canal for their holidays.

202.   A lorry pictured during the 1930s. It belonged to William Simmons, miller, The Mill, Mill Road. This celebrated flour was used for making bread and pastry.

203.   *F. W. Buckmaster, motor and electrical engineer who had a garage and cars for hire, 16 North Street. Pictured during the 1930s.*

204.   *1920s picture of Harry Hunt's motor garage with one of his hire cars. The garage was situated next to the* Bedford Arms, Linslade.

Special Events

Leighton Buzzard has found many excuses to celebrate ranging from national occasions to singularly odd local customs.

The town used to celebrate the anniversary of the restoration of Charles II. On the 29 May every year (Oak Apple Day), oak boughs used to be placed in the upper lights of the spire of All Saints Church and the church bells were rung.

In order to celebrate the wedding of Edward VII, then Prince of Wales, to Princess Alexandria, the town hired a 'professional ox-roaster' from Shipston-on-Stowe, Worcestershire. The ox was brought from London and paraded through the town on the afternoon of Friday, 6 March 1863, adorned with rosettes and colours and watched by half the town.

The ox was roasted the following Monday night near the Town Hall. By 10 am the following morning the ox was ready and the first slice was carved. For the children there was plum pudding. After a parade in the afternoon they gave three cheers for the Queen, the Committee, the Vicar and 'Old England', before disappearing to consume their 672 pounds of plum pudding. In the evening a torchlight procession was organised by the fire brigade. A tradesman's ball was also held in the Assembly Rooms.

The most unusual custom that still survives is the Rogation Monday service which originated in 1693. The service starts at All Saints Church and finishes at the Wilkes' Almshouses where a portion of the will of Edward Wilkes is read out while a choirboy or girl stands on their head.

This custom dates back to when the land was unenclosed and boundaries needed to be regularly marked out so that younger generations should not forget them. The service has been held every year since 1693 following directions laid down in the will of Matthew Wilkes. His father Edward built the almshouses in 1630 and Matthew left funds to be used solely for the annual commemoration on Rogation Monday.

A procession of clergy, trustees and clerk of the Wilkes charity, churchwardens, choirboys and girls, crucifer and garland bearer start from All Saints Church and make their way through the High Street and along North Street to arrive at the almshouses by noon. Prayers are said before the clerk of the trustees reads an extract from the will of Edward Wilkes. In accordance with tradition a choirboy or girl stands on their head in order to impress upon their mind the object of the proceedings. The occupants of the almshouses are each given 50p (10s originally), as part of the tradition.

The procession then heads towards the Market Cross where the children enjoy lemonade and sticky buns. After this event a barbeque is held in the churchyard.

In earlier times, when the service was over, buns and beer were given away outside the *Swan Hotel*. The beer was discontinued in 1860 and from 1877 to 1897 buns were given out in the schools. It was also a custom that after the service the widow occupants of the almshouses together with the town-crier and sexton would have dinner and tea at the *Swan Hotel*. The trustees would also dine together there.

205. *Water and sewage works ceremony, 1896. The occasion was the laying of the foundation stone at the water tower in Stanbridge Road, by W. Page. Beside the tower was the town's cattle pond, into which passing drovers penned their cattle if they could not reach their destination in daylight.*

206. *Election meeting, 1890s outside the* Swan Hotel. *Col Oliver Thomas Duke is seen here on a stagecoach addressing a crowd of electors. He lived in Heath and Reach and in 1892 and 1895 was the unsuccessful Tory candidate for South Bedfordshire.*

207.   9 August 1902. Celebration of the Coronation of King Edward VII and peace celebrations to mark the end of the Boer War. The hitching posts, normally used to tether cattle, have been used to anchor evergreen boughs and between them were looped festoons. The Beds Imperial Yeomanry can be seen parading down the High Street heading a tableau of Kings and Queens of England.

208.   Public meeting by the Market Cross held Thursday, 5 October 1905 to celebrate the release from Bedford jail of the Revs John W. Mayo (Baptist), John Bowles and Arthur Roberts (Primitive Methodist). They were jailed for seven days because they had not paid their respective portion of the Poor Rate (Education Rate). Rev Mayo and Rev Roberts both owed 6s 8d while Rev Bowles was 8s 2d in arrears. They were against payment of the rate because it was used to pay for education in sectarian schools, where doctrines were taught to which they could not subscribe. The Rev J. W. Harrison presided at this meeting and after speeches by the three ministers, Dr Clifford gave a rousing address.

209–210.   *British School Old Boys Commemoration Day, 13 July 1905, by the Market Cross. A local photographer is standing on a step-ladder in order to take the picture seen (below).*

211.   A French 'Moto-Bloc' 16hp hire car, 25cwt, registration A1 FM, was in collision on Monday evening, 14 August 1905 with a Wolsey 24hp motor trolley on the Watling Street (A5), midway between Hockliffe and Dunstable near the Tilsworth turning. The car, pictured above, was overtaking the trolley at about 20 mph when their wheels caught and the car overturned. The trolley was travelling at less than the regulation speed of 8 mph allowed for this type of vehicle. Sadly, the driver of the car, Mrs Hawnt, aged about 30, died in the accident. This postcard was posted just three days after the accident.

212.   First Armistice Day Service, 1919, held by the Market Cross. Scouts stand guard over the memorial.

213.   *Erecting the war memorial, 1920. Two huge baulks of timber one foot square and 30 feet long were erected either side of the base to form a derrick. The work took three days to complete. A lead tube containing coins was placed in a bolthole in the base of the monument by Harry Yirrell and Fletcher Brotherton.*

214.   *Second anniversary of Armistice, 11 November 1920. Over 5,000 people crowded into Church Square and High Street to see the unveiling of the war memorial by Lord Ampthill. After his speech, in which he said that the most pitiable sight of all was an 'ex-soldier begging for his bread', there was a short silence, Lord Ampthill then saluted the monument and the vicar of Leighton gave a dedication. The service finished with a hymn and the last post. Throughout the service four uniformed ex-officers, one of them blind, stood at each corner of the memorial.*

215.   *Unveiling of the war memorial Linslade, 11 November 1920, in memory of the 41 people killed during the 1914–18 war. Being independent, both towns had their own memorials and separate services.*

216.   *Meeting by the Market Cross, taken by local photographer P. J. Baker. Union Jacks are in abundance and several local organisations are present. The banners of the Leighton Primitive Methodist Church, Wesleyan Church and Hockliffe Road Baptist School can be seen.*

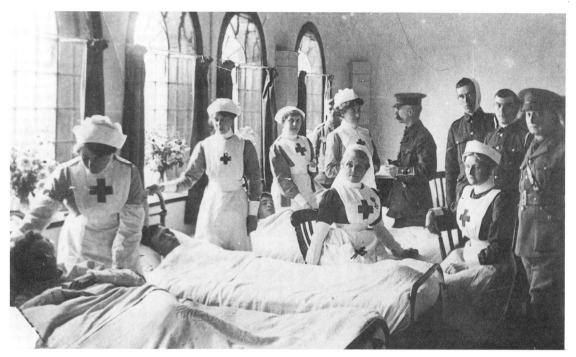

217. *The workhouse, being used as a hospital during the 1914–18 war. Nurse Ericson is seated (left).*

218. *Leighton's first ambulance, run by garage owner Frank R. Webb, comes to the end of its working life after being crushed by a tree. Luckily no one was injured, as this was before the National Health Service and one had to pay to be taken to hospital. Before the introduction of the motor ambulance, transport was by horse and cab or by being pushed in a hand stretcher. The picture was taken about 1925.*

219. *Ox Roast, Bailey's Field, Lake Street. The newly-elected MP for mid-Bedfordshire is carving, November 1931. The event was held to celebrate the election of Alan Lennox-Boyd, Conservative MP. Nearly all the townspeople went along to collect their free slice of prime beef and bread.*

220. *Royal Scot train crash, Sunday, 22 March 1931. The express train was travelling from Euston to Glasgow when the driver failed to observe a slow signal. The train crossed from the fast track to the slow one at 60 mph instead of 15 mph. Fouling the points the train crashed 200 yards south of the wooden footbridge near the railway station. Local people rushed to the scene of the accident to help. Amazingly only 5 people died including the driver and fireman. All four tracks were closed for 24 hours while the wreckage was cleared.*

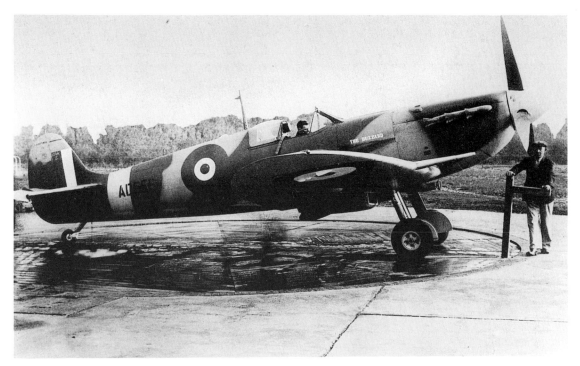

221. 'The Buzzard', a Spitfire VB with Merlin 32 engine, RAF No AD 556, which was presented to the Ministry of Aircraft Production by Leighton Buzzard, Linslade and Rural District of Wing during War Weapons Week, 1941. Some of the money raised to pay for the aircraft came from charging people to look at a shot-down Messerschmitt in the grounds of the then Cedars Grammar School.

222. Queuing for fish outside Bardell Brothers, fishmongers, 32 High Street during the 1939–45 war.

223.   *Fatstock Show, Church Square, 13 December 1949. The show, which was first held in the late 19th century, was arranged in the High Street and Church Square with table poultry and eggs exhibited in the Corn Exchange. A celebration dinner afterwards was held at the* Swan Hotel. *This Christmas show was the first for 11 years which Chamber of Trade president J. J. Hopkins said made everybody feel the town 'was on the map'. The fair was moved soon after to the Sale Yard because it became too costly to erect the posts and barriers which were used to restrain the animals and because labour was in short supply.*

224.   *On Sunday, 21 May 1950 a tornado caused the lights in a Leighton church to go out just as they reached a reference to light in the hymn. But many local people will remember it as they day when their roofs were damaged and their houses and gardens flooded. Hailstones the size of pigeon eggs rained down on Leighton as the tornado swept on its way. Television aerials in Plantation Road were described as 'looking like corkscrews'. One man who saw some of his poultry minus their feathers said: 'They looked just about ready for Christmas.'*

225–226. The etching (above), from a photograph by local photographer W. H. Piggott, appeared in the Leighton Buzzard Observer on 19 May 1896. Since 1693, on Rogation Monday, a procession of clergy, churchwardens, choirboys and girls, trustees and clerk of the Wilkes charity have arrived at the almshouses, North Street, at noon. The picture (below) taken in 1985 shows Peter Richardson, the clerk to the trustees reading an extract from the will of Edward Wilkes, who bequeathed funds to maintain the almshouses. In accordance with tradition a choirboy or girl stands on his or her head 'in order that he or she may understand and retain the words better'. Choirgirl, Heidi Shillitto, aged 11, can be seen standing on her head supported by the Rev Whittaker.

Crime

Little is known about crime in Leighton Buzzard prior to the 16th century as written records are very scarce. The Bedfordshire Sessions minute books for the years 1649–60 contains only four references to Leighton, which is a very good record for the town.

At the Bedfordshire Sessions held 26 April 1652 it is recorded that Elizabeth Lee and Thomas Lee of Billington were ordered to be whipped for stealing a lamb, colour white, price 11d.

In 1659–60 two cases of sheep stealing in the county are recorded for which the capital sentence might have been carried out. However, in both cases the accused pleaded 'benefit of clergy' (first offence) and were 'cauterized' (branded) and discharged.

In 1786 Henry Sanders was committed for running away and leaving his wife chargeable to the parish of Leighton Buzzard. He was ordered to be publicly whipped at Bedford and given six months' hard labour. Upon finishing his sentence he was to be taken to Leighton Buzzard and publicly whipped before being discharged.

A three-month term of imprisonment was given in 1861 to a 15-year-old girl for stealing a loaf of bread. The Bench considered that her education had been sadly neglected and that she might learn some household duties during her stay in prison.

Local people will remember the following five crimes that were front-page headlines during this century.

Miss Ruby Keen was found murdered in April 1937 on Firs Path off Plantation Road. A special edition newspaper priced a halfpenny was produced in Leighton to cover the murder story. A local man was soon arrested and subsequently convicted. This was the first case in Leighton Buzzard where forensic science was used to convict a killer. The murderer was Leslie Stone, a Heath man, who was hanged on Friday, 13 August 1937. He has the dubious honour of being the last person from this area to be hanged.

In March 1975 a 76-year-old widow, Elsie Claydon was found dead by her brother-in-law Robert Claydon. He had walked the short distance from the cottage they both shared to the *Railway Hotel* for a drink. Upon returning home at about 10.30 pm he found the back door open. Realising something was wrong he entered the cottage and found his sister-in-law's bloody and battered body lying on the bed. She had been stabbed repeatedly in the head, the body and the legs.

This case like that of Carol Morgan, who was murdered in 1981, is still unsolved. Mrs Morgan kept a small corner shop near Finch Crescent. While her husband and two children were at the cinema she was battered to death by a mad axeman. A witness making a call from a telephone box in Cedars Way saw the suspect, a white youth aged about 21 carrying two plastic bags, drop some money on the ground before getting into a dark green Ford Cortina Estate.

During the summer of 1984 a man known as 'The Fox' committed a series of burglaries, rapes and sex attacks on men and women. For a period of four months he terrorised the area around Leighton Buzzard. When he was sentenced, Malcolm Fairley received three life sentences for rape and three life sentences for aggravated burglary. He also received various sentences ranging from two years for indecent assault to 14 years for burglary.

The Great Train Robbery is often referred to 'as the crime of the century' and it certainly put Linslade on the map.

On Thursday, 8 August 1963, just after 3 o'clock in the morning, fifteen masked men held up the night train from Glasgow to London near Bridego Bridge situated between Linslade and Cheddington. By using a glove to cover the green light and placing a light behind the red signal the train driver was tricked into stopping the train. He was then coshed and overpowered. The robbers next uncoupled the engine and front two coaches from the rest of the train. The injured driver was then ordered to shunt the train half-a-mile to Bridego Bridge.

The 128 mail bags containing £2,631,684 were easily thrown over the parapet bridge into a waiting Austin army lorry. This truck together with two Landrovers were parked in a lay-by next to a pond used by fishermen.

The train robbers then journeyed 27 miles to their hideout at Leatherslade Farm, near Brill in Buckinghamshire. Their route had been carefully worked out so as to avoid using major roads or large towns and led through the villages of Wingrave, Aston Abbots, Cublington, Whitchurch, Oving, Pitchcott, Upper Winchendon and Chilton.

Scotland Yard relentlessly pursued the gang and within one month several arrests had been made. The robbers were brought to Linslade Magistrate's Court on the Wing Road where they were remanded in custody for trial at Aylesbury Assize Court. Amongst them was the now famous Ronnie Biggs. He along with Charlie Wilson eventually escaped from prison and fled abroad with other members of the gang.

In 1968 Charlie Wilson was arrested in Canada by the Royal Canadian Mounted Police and flown back to London. In the same year another member of the gang, Bruce Reynolds was arrested in Torquay. The only known member of the gang to remain free was Ronnie Biggs.

227.   *Bridego Bridge, scene of the Great Train Robbery. On Thursday 8 August 1963, just after 3 am, a gang of masked men held up the night train from Glasgow to London and stole over £2½ million, mainly in used notes. They were being returned to the Bank of England for destruction. The driver was severely injured by the robbers. Over £2 million of the stolen money is still missing.*

228.   *Part of the old police station in Wing Road which had three cells, an inspector's house and a police court. It was to this court that the train robbers were brought, to be remanded in custody for trial at Aylesbury. This building has now been converted into private flats.*

10044/PC10001
SAWN-OFF SHOTGUN

10050/DAK10001 LEFT
HAND GAUNTLETT

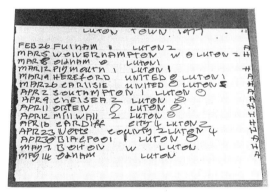

229–231.   *Exhibits displayed at the police station open day, 5 May 1985. The exhibits, a sawn-off shotgun, gauntlet and handwriting sample were used in the prosecution of Malcolm Fairley, the masked raider and rapist nicknamed 'The Fox', who terrorised this area during the summer of 1984. He began his life of crime as a petty thief and went on to become feared by residents throughout South Bedfordshire. A massive police hunt was launched and he was eventually tracked down to his home in Kentish Town. Fairley was jailed for life for his many crimes which included a sex attack on a young woman in the village of Edlesborough.*

Surrounding Area

Leighton Buzzard is surrounded by the villages of Billington, Eggington, Heath and Reach and Stanbridge. Other nearby places include Hockliffe, Mentmore, Soulbury and Wing. Ascott House and its gardens attract many visitors, while the *Three Locks*, situated on the Bletchley Road, provides an attractive spot to sit and watch the narrow boats pass by.

Billington is a small village with a population of 377. The village has several thatched cottages and a 13th century church. It is situated to the south-east of Leighton and from its hilltop position enjoys fine views of the countryside.

Eggington is a small agricultural village and with its hamlet of Clipstone it is situated in the south-west corner of Bedfordshire, between Leighton Buzzard and the A5. In the main street are two chapels and a church but its principal feature is the classical Eggington House. There is no village shop as this was closed some time ago. When the local school was threatened with closure in 1983, a village newsletter called the 'Eggington Pump' was started by Harry and Linda Sear. The newsletter could not save the school but enough support was generated for the building to be turned into a small village hall. Today the hall helps keep the community spirit alive by providing a meeting place for groups like the WI and Young Farmers' drama group.

Heath and Reach with a population of 1,369 lies to the north of Leighton Buzzard. It is surrounded by sand workings and woodlands. One of the woodland areas open to the public, and which is well worth a visit, is Stockgrove Country Park on the Great Brickhill Road. The village has a small church with a short tower, dating from the 16th century when Heath was a hamlet of Leighton Buzzard. In 1906 some of the principal inhabitants were: George Bates (miller and farmer), Albert Cherry (coal dealer), John Haybittle (schoolmaster) and James Jabez Rayner (wheelwright).

Stanbridge with a population of 827 is situated between Leighton Buzzard and Dunstable. The parish church of St John the Baptist overlooks the village green. Although the church has been restored it still contains an Early English font. In 1876 some prominent people living in the village were: Charles Birdsey (tailor), Arthur Bunker (butcher); William E. Costin (carpenter), Joseph Eames (*Five Bells*), Samuel Tims (straw plait merchant), William Tompkins (blacksmith) and Josiah Wilks (shopkeeper). A windmill stands on a hill overlooking the village. It was in use until the end of the 19th century but has now been converted into a house. In 1983 several additional rooms were designed by architect Graham Weatherley. A lounge, study, kitchen and utility room were added, with curved walls to match the existing building. In 1985 the 42-foot-high listed building was offered for sale at £150,000.

Hockliffe, situated on the ancient Watling Street (A5), was once known as 'Hockley in the Hill'. During the 18th century it consisted of a long row of houses, mostly coaching inns. One such inn was the *White Horse* which is now privately owned by Michael Stray who uses the building for his business of restoring fireplaces and wooden furniture. On the front of the building are some wooden carvings believed to have been taken from the old Toddington Manor.

Mentmore is situated south-west of Leighton and owes its existence to the Rothschild family. It has an extremely attractive village green. People remember Mentmore not only for Mentmore Towers but for the impressive *Stag Inn* run by the only French licensee in Britain.

Soulbury village is situated some three miles north-west of Leighton. It has a large village green and attractive thatched cottages and there are also several monuments to the Lovett family of nearby Liscombe Park.

Wing is situated some three miles south-west of Leighton. The parish church of All Saints is the best preserved Saxon church in the country where a Saxon apse and crypt may still be seen. A 'castle mound' is present in the village but whether there was ever a castle here remains a matter for debate. In 1969 the village offered fierce opposition to the proposed siting of the third London Airport in the Cublington, Stewkley and Wing area. The Wing Airport Resistance Association was formed and the 'Wings Off Wing' campaign was a great success. Since then the population of the village has increased by nearly 50 per cent and now stands at 2,718.

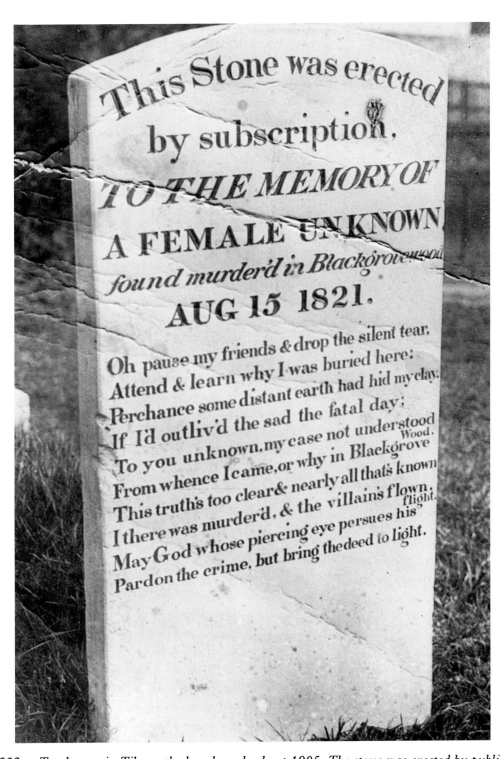

This Stone was erected by subscription, TO THE MEMORY OF A FEMALE UNKNOWN found murder'd in Blackgrove wood AUG 15 1821.

Oh pause my friends & drop the silent tear,
Attend & learn why I was buried here:
Perchance some distant earth had hid my clay.
If I'd outliv'd the sad the fatal day;
To you unknown, my case not understood
From whence I came, or why in Blackgrove Wood.
This truth's too clear & nearly all thats known
I there was murder'd, & the villain's flown; flight.
May God whose piercing eye persues his
Pardon the crime, but bring the deed to light.

232.   *Tombstone in Tilsworth churchyard, about 1905. The stone was erected by public subscription for a murder victim who was found dead in Blackgrove Wood, 15 August 1821. In order to remove the body a stable door was taken off its hinges and used to transport the body to Wood Farm. The victim was never identified and the murderer never caught.*

233.   *Stanbridge School Class, Group III, 1922.*

234.   *Stanbridge School with headmaster Mr Delamont and pupils standing by the gate.*

235. *Football team, Stanbridge. Headmaster, Mr Delamont (left) with the players who include: W. Cooper, M. Blake, S. Bunker and Mr Price.*

236. *The* Five Bells, *Stanbridge, about 1913. The name on the notice above the door reads 'Philip Olney' and the sign on the side advertises 'fine home brewed ale'. Chickens are running around in the foreground. The landlord, Mr Olney used to sell clay pipes. These were used for smoking by the men and bubble blowing by the children.*

237.   *A deserted Watling Street, Hockliffe early 1900s. The road was originally built by the Romans. Their roads were long and straight and the military staging posts like Dunstable and St Albans were one day's walking distance apart, about 12 miles. The White Hart (right) is advertised as a 'cyclists house' and is situated at the corner of the road leading to Leighton Buzzard.*

238.   *In 1932 a new White Hart was built in the style of a Swiss chalet. This 1930s picture was taken when it was a hotel and the proprietor was A. Greatorex. Recently the premises have been completely refurbished as a Beefeater restaurant and pub, with the interior in the new rustic style.*

239. *Chalk Hill Cutting, A5, Dunstable, 1928. Before the cutting was made, Puddle Hill (right) was joined with Maidenbower (left). A man is walking in the middle of the road towards the horse and cart. It would be impossible to walk along this busy main road today.*

240. *Heath village, about 1916. Behind the horse and cart is the clock tower and well-house, erected by subscription in 1873. The cost of the clock was met by Baroness Burdett Coutts and Baroness de Rothschild. The pump was presented by Mr Brantom in memory of William Abraham. A four-foot diameter wheel was used to draw the water from the well.*

241. *Wing village hall pictured shortly after opening in 1906. The hall was built as a memorial to Charles Coates and was opened by Lord Rothschild in January 1906. The building was designed by the architect J. J. Heady.*

242. *All Saints Church, Wing. This Saxon church is believed to have been built in the 7th century and has been described as the most important church in the county. In the church are splendid memorials to the Dormer family. The church is one of only three in the country which has a Saxon apse and crypt.*

243. *The entrance, Mentmore Towers, about 1919. The house was designed by Sir Joseph Paxton who designed the Crystal Palace. It is thought to have been the first modern house in England to have central heating installed. This luxurious house was built for Mayer Amschal Rothschild and finally completed in 1855. In 1878 his daughter, Hannah Rothschild, married the Earl of Roseberry who later became Prime Minister. The art collections at Mentmore were once amongst the most outstanding of their kind anywhere in the world. In the 1970s the contents of the house were auctioned. The building itself was acquired by the 'World Government of the Age of Enlightenment'.*

244. *Soulbury village green with the house known locally as the 'Thatchies'. Dean Farm Lane is to the left of the house and car. Photograph about 1923.*

Local Clubs and Societies

The following is a list of a few of the local clubs and societies to be found in Leighton–Linslade. The Library and Arts Centre, Lake Street keeps a comprehensive list of the clubs and societies in South Bedfordshire.

Leighton Buzzard Chess Club
Leighton Buzzard Computer Club
Leighton-Linslade Flower Club
Leighton Buzzard Model Boats and Car Club
Leighton-Linslade Model Railway Club
Leighton and Linslade Wine Circle
Leighton Buzzard Bridge Club
Country & Western Club
Leighton Buzzard Photography Club
Leighton-Linslade Radio Club
Leighton Buzzard Stamp Club
Linsleighders Folk Dance Society
Linslade Horticultural Society
Leighton Buzzard Children's Book Group

Arena Children's Theatre
Leighton Buzzard Drama Group
North Street Players
Vandyke Film Society
Vandyke Jazz Club
Leighton Buzzard Music Club
Leighton Masqueraders
Leighton-Linslade Amateur Operatic Society
Tolkien Society
Leighton Buzzard Arts Society
Heath Band
Eaton Bray Choral Society
Leighton Buzzard Festival Singers
Linslade Singers

Leighton Buzzard Athletic Club
Leighton Buzzard Angling Club
Brooklands Badminton Club
Buzzard Badminton Club
Eaton Bray Badminton Club

Leighton Linslade Badminton Club
Plantation Badminton Club
Leighton Buzzard Bowling Club
Linslade Bowls Club
Leighton Buzzard Canoe Club
Eggington Cricket Club
Leighton Buzzard Cricket and Tennis Club
Linslade Cricket Team
Brooklands Cricket Club
Linslade Cricket Club
Leighton Athletic Football Club
Leighton Town Football Club
The Knolls Squash Club
Leighton Buzzard Hockey Club
Leighton Buzzard Kung-Fu Club
Leighton Buzzard Table Tennis League
Leighton Buzzard Tennis and Cricket Club
Linslade Tennis Club
Leighton Buzzard Rugby Football Club

Leighton-Linslade Townswomen's Guild
Inner Wheel Club
Leighton Buzzard Ladies Circle
St Barnabas Wives Fellowship Club
Linslade Women's Institute
Leighton Buzzard Knife and Fork Club
Leighton Buzzard Vegetarian Society

Barnacles Club
Girls Brigade Company
Group 20
Leighton Buzzard Pre-School Play Group Association
Rotaract Club
Leighton Buzzard and District Scouts
18 Plus Group

WRVS Darby and Joan Club
Leighton-Linslade Old People's Welfare Association
Civil Service Retirement Fellowship
Leighton-Linslade Retirement Group

Leighton-Linslade Deaf Club
Leighton Buzzard Partially Sighted and Blind Club
Leighton Buzzard Club for Physically Handicapped
Disabled Sports Club

Leighton-Linslade Chamber of Trade & Commerce
Leighton Buzzard Crime Prevention Panel
Brooklands Residents Association
Central Linslade Residents Association
Leighton-Linslade Carnival Committee
Leighton Buzzard Licensed Victuallers Association
Lions International
Mad Hatters
New Zealand Reunion Club
Old Cedarians Association
Leighton Buzzard Peace Campaign
Rotary Club of Leighton Buzzard
Leighton Buzzard and District Round Table

South Beds & District Farmers Club
Chiltern Friendship Club
Spanish Club of Leighton Buzzard
Leighton-Linslade Town Twinning Association
Workers Educational Association
Leighton Buzzard & District Canal Club
Knolls Wood Protection Society
Leighton Buzzard Preservation Society

Index

Sources of Photographs

The following list of the sources and original publishers (where known) of the pictures:

Anderson Photography   6, 10, 12, 17, 31, 37, 62, 106, 108, 118, 124, 136–139, 142–144, 146, 149, 157, 163–164, 168, 207, 209, 215, 221.

Author   23, 29, 67–68, 127, 135, 151, 175–177, 179–181, 200, 227–231, 242.

A. J. Bacon   238.

Bacons   63.

P. J. Baker   11, 20–21, 43, 174, 199, 216.

Mrs H. Batchelar   91.

Bedfordshire County Council Photographic Unit   36, 41, 52–53, 123.

Bedfordshire County Record Office   24, 30, 38, 40, 44, 65–66, 69, 71–85, 158, 206, 210.

Beds and Bucks Observer   100, 102, 183, 190, 194, 224.

Bell   26.

F. W. Bendy   32, 110.

Buckinghamshire County Museum   59–60, 130–131, 160, 243.

Buckinghamshire County Record Office   58, 150.

L. Cooper   101, 120, 140, 161, 197, 211, 232–236, 241.

F. Frith and Co   201.

E. Hillsdon   166–167.

H. Jackson   48, 51, 70, 125, 148.

Kingsway   14, 28, 56, 240.

T. Lawson   16, 18, 25, 49, 86–90, 92–100, 103, 126, 134, 155, 159, 165, 169, 171–173, 186–189, 193, 195, 202–204, 212–214, 217–220, 222.

Leighton Buzzard Narrow Gauge Railway Society   170, 191–192.

Lloyd, Linslade   7, 54, 59–60, 133.

Lloyd and Son   39.

Frank Lloyd   132.

Luton Museum and Art Gallery   5, 15, 35, 42, 46, 47, 61, 64, 105, 109, 112–113, 114–115, 122, 141, 152, 154, 156, 178, 185, 198, 205, 223.

P. N. Series   27.

W. F. Piggott   40, 153, 208.

Real Photo Series   182.

Rush and Warwick   22, 237.

Raphael Tuck and Sons   104.

Valentine   13, 19.

The Waterways Museum   3–4, 162.

W. H. S. and S.   184.

Rev P. H. Whittaker   45, 145

Subscribers

Paul Anthony Charles ANGHINETTI
Mr P. W. ARIS
Sue AYLING
Hilda Muriel BATCHELAR
John BATTLE
BEDFORDSHIRE COUNTY COUNCIL
   LIBRARIES
Margaret BIRCHALL
Helen & Keith BLACKWELL
BODLEIAN LIBRARY, OXFORD
Jonathan D. BRADBURY
BRITISH LIBRARY
Ann BROOKES
Sheila BULTEEL
CEDARS UPPER SCHOOL
Sylvie, Serge, Stephanie & Steve CHOJNACKI
Edwin CLARKE
Gloria CLARKE
E. & M. COLLINS
C. W. COPCUTT
Mr C. D. CORNWELL
COUNTY RECORD OFFICE, BEDFORD
Stephen DANCE
Christine DANIELS
W. F. DENTON
Colin DIMMOCK
DOVERY DOWN LOWER SCHOOL
Leslie Richard EVANS
Kathleen FARNON
Jacqueline FARRELL
E. FISHER
W. A. FITTON
D. FOOKES
J. Mark FREEMAN
Mr & Mrs F. J. FRENCH
Michael R. GELL
Dorothy GERMANN
GILBERT INGLEFIELD MIDDLE SCHOOL
H. J. GOODYEAR
John GOUT
J. & T. HANCOCK
Lisa HARRIS
Kathryn M. HART
Priscilla & David HART
Robert D. P. HART
Dr V. E. LLOYD HART
Justine, Emma & Charlotte HARWOOD
Joyce HAYS
John A. HAZELL
Colin & Val HEMSLEY
David P. HILLIER
Mr & Mrs H. T. HOBBS
A. & R. HODEY
Eileen HOLMES
W. T. HOLTON
Mr B. M. INNS
Ken & Sandra JONES
S. A. JONES

Mrs Amanda JOVIC
Charles Michael KAYE
Barbara KEELEY
Glen D. KITCHEN
Alan KNOWLES
Julia KNOWLES
Kim & Colin LAMBERT
Tom LAWSON
LEIGHTON MIDDLE SCHOOL
LIBRARY OF TRINITY COLLEGE,
   DUBLIN
LINSLADE MIDDLE SCHOOL
LUTON MUSEUM & ART GALLERY
Kathryn MARTIN
The MILLS FAMILY
Peter, Linda, Brian & Tracy MOORE
Mary & Ron MOUNTFORT
John NASH
NATIONAL LIBRARY OF SCOTLAND
NATIONAL LIBRARY OF WALES
Anthea & David PHILLIPS
Derek PLATER
Val & Stu POLLARD
K. PRATT
Mrs Carole PRINCE
Gillian REDWAY
Nick & Sue RICHARDS
P. A. D. RICHARDSON
Dave & Julie ROBINSON
ST GEORGE'S SCHOOL
Alan SCOTT
Beryl & Harold SHELDON
W. G. SHELFORD
Thomas H. SHEPHERD
Mrs P. SHIRLEY
Andrew SIMMONDS
Ian & Jill SKUDDER
Valerie SMALL
Bernard & Emily SMITH
E. G. SMITH
Jenny SMITH
Mary STRODE (née WHEELER)
John J. SULLIVAN
Chris SZCZEPANSKI
Janet TARBOX
John E. TARBOX
A. D. TAYLOR
UNIVERSITY LIBRARY, CAMBRIDGE
John VICKERS
M. J. WAPLES
Ronald WELLS
Victor WHITEMORE
VIV & JEAN WILLIS
WING COUNTY SECONDARY SCHOOL
Tom, Janet, Neil & Jenna WISE
Michael J. WOODWARDS
Thomas YATES